CUTTING EDGE

STARTER

WORKBOOK

peter moor chris redston

Contents

Module 7

Module 8

Module 9

Module 10

Module 11

Module 12

Names and introductions

1 **a)** Complete the sentences with *I*, *my*, *you* or *your*.

1 Hello, ..*I*.. 'm Roy Magee.

2 A: Are .... Teresa Daley?

3 Hello. What's .... name?

4 A: Hello, ... name's Frank.
B: Hi, ... 'm Paola. Nice to meet ....

b) Listen and check.

Vocabulary: jobs; *a/an*

2 Write the letters and *a* or *an*.

a) *a* w *a* i t *e* r
b) __ d _ c t _ r
c) __ s t _ d _ n t
d) __ a _ t _ r
e) __ b _ s _ n _ s s m _ n
f) __ _ n g _ n _ _ r
g) __ p _ l _ c _ _ f f _ c _ r
h) __ t _ _ c h _ r

he/she/his/her

3 **a)** Complete the sentences with *He*, *His*, *She* or *Her*.

1 ...*His*... first name is Sean.
2 .... full name is Sean Adrian Cowley.
3 .... 's an actor.
4 .... 's a student.
5 .... full name is Monica Adriana Vega.

6 .... first name is Carole.
7 .... full name is Carole Jane Miller.
8 .... 's a businesswoman.
9 .... full name is Michael Eric Thompson.
10 .... 's a police officer.

b) Listen and check.

I/my/you/your/his/her

4

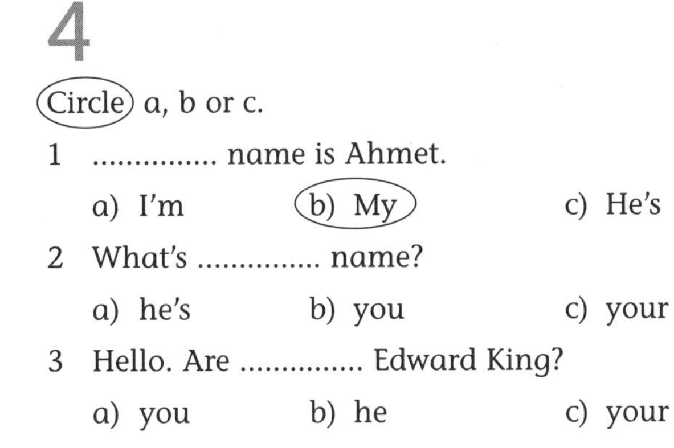

Circle a, b or c.

1 .... name is Ahmet.
a) I'm b) My c) He's

2 What's .... name?
a) he's b) you c) your

3 Hello. Are .... Edward King?
a) you b) he c) your

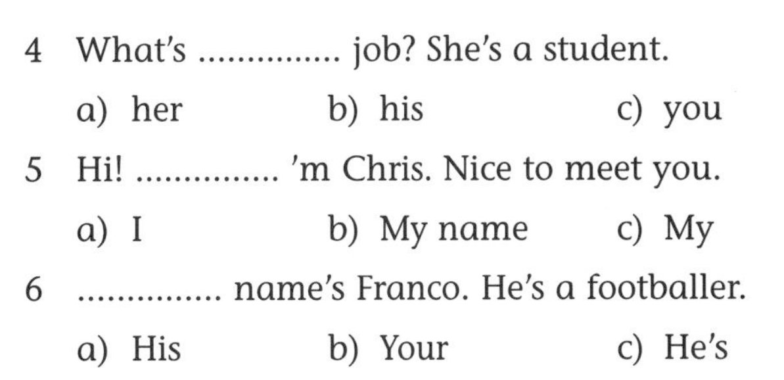

4 What's .... job? She's a student.
a) her b) his c) you

5 Hi! .... 'm Chris. Nice to meet you.
a) I b) My name c) My

6 .... name's Franco. He's a footballer.
a) His b) Your c) He's

Pronunciation

5 Listen and say these words and phrases.

a) I

b) I'm

c) hi!

d) fine

e) nice

f) my

The alphabet; *How do you spell ...?*

6 Write the names of the famous people. Listen and check.

a)

NEIL ARMSTRONG

b)

_AT__R_NE _ET_-_ON__

c)

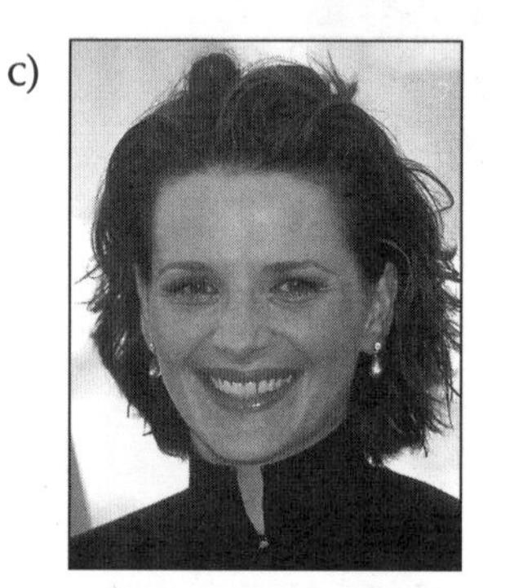

_U_I_T _I_O__E

d)

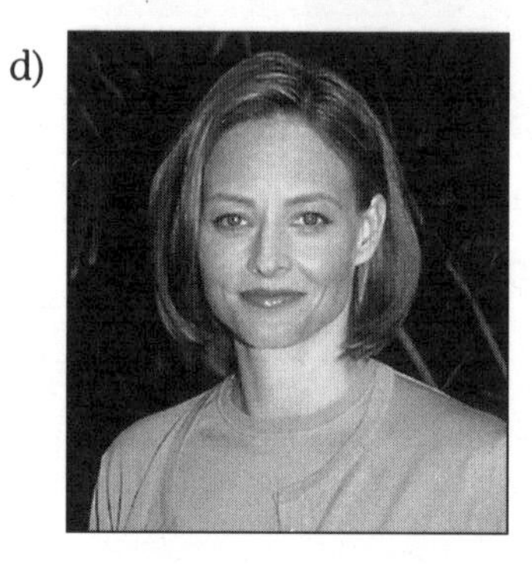

_OD__ _OST__

e)

_UE_T_N T_R_N_IN_

f)

_E__N S__C_Y

7 **a)** Write the questions.

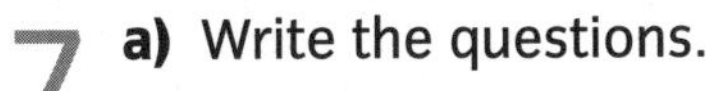

Simon Kenley *Mary Ann Hazinger*

1	..*What's his*... first name?	Simon.
2	.... surname?	Kenley
3	.... spell that?	K - E - N - L - E - Y
4	.... name?	Mary
5	.... name?	Mary Ann Hazinger

b) Listen and check.

Numbers 0–20

8 **a)** Write the numbers.

three	....*3*....	six	....
eleven	....	eighteen	....
nine	....	ten	....
seventeen	....	four	....
twelve	....	five	....

b) Spell the numbers.

1	....*one*....	16	....
7	....	14	....
8	....	20	....
13	....	15	....
2	....	19	....

Improve your writing

Full stops, question marks

? = question mark **.** = full stop

9 Write **?** or **.** in the circles.

a) 'What's your name ⓘ?'
'My name's Natalia ◯.'

b) 'Are you Anna Schmidt ◯'
'No, I'm Barbara Schmidt ◯'

c) 'Hi, Sonja! How are you ◯'
'I'm fine ◯ And you ◯'

d) 'What's her surname ◯'

e) 'His name's Jan Talich ◯ He's a doctor ◯'

f) 'What's your job ◯'
'I'm a singer ◯'

Capital letters (1)

10

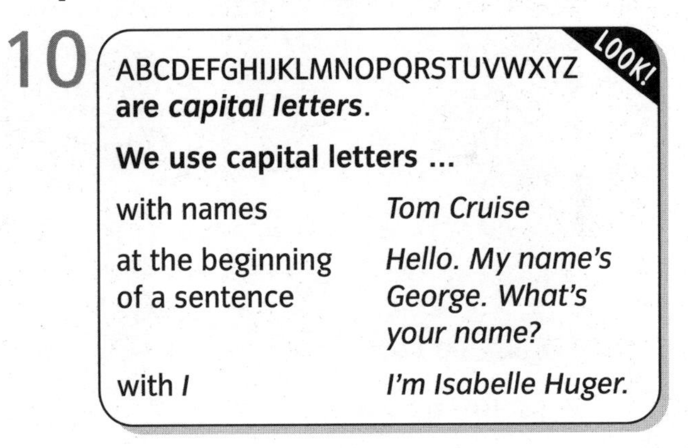

LOOK!

ABCDEFGHIJKLMNOPQRSTUVWXYZ
are *capital letters*.

We use capital letters ...

with names	*Tom Cruise*
at the beginning of a sentence	*Hello. My name's George. What's your name?*
with *I*	*I'm Isabelle Huger.*

Write the sentences with capital letters.

a) ~~h~~*H*is name's Tony. ~~h~~*H*e's an actor.

b) johnny depp is an actor.

c) her name is jennifer jones. she's a singer.

d) A: 'what's your name?'
B: 'my name's andrea.'

e) 'hello, abdul, how are you?' 'i'm fine.'

f) my name's istvan and i'm an engineer.

Listen and read

Real names

11 Listen and read. Who is Caryn Johnson?

■ **Bono is the singer in the group U2. His real name is Paul Hewson.**

■ **Stephen King is an American writer. But Stephen King isn't his real name: his first name is Richard, and his surname is Bachman.**

■ **She's an American actress ... but Demi Moore is not her real name. Her real name is Demetria Guynes.**

■ **Sting is an English musician and singer, but his real name is Gordon Matthew Sumner.**

■ **Her real surname is Johnson ... and Caryn is her real first name. She's an American actress. What's her name? ***

* Whoopi Goldberg

module 2

Vocabulary: countries

1 Write the country.

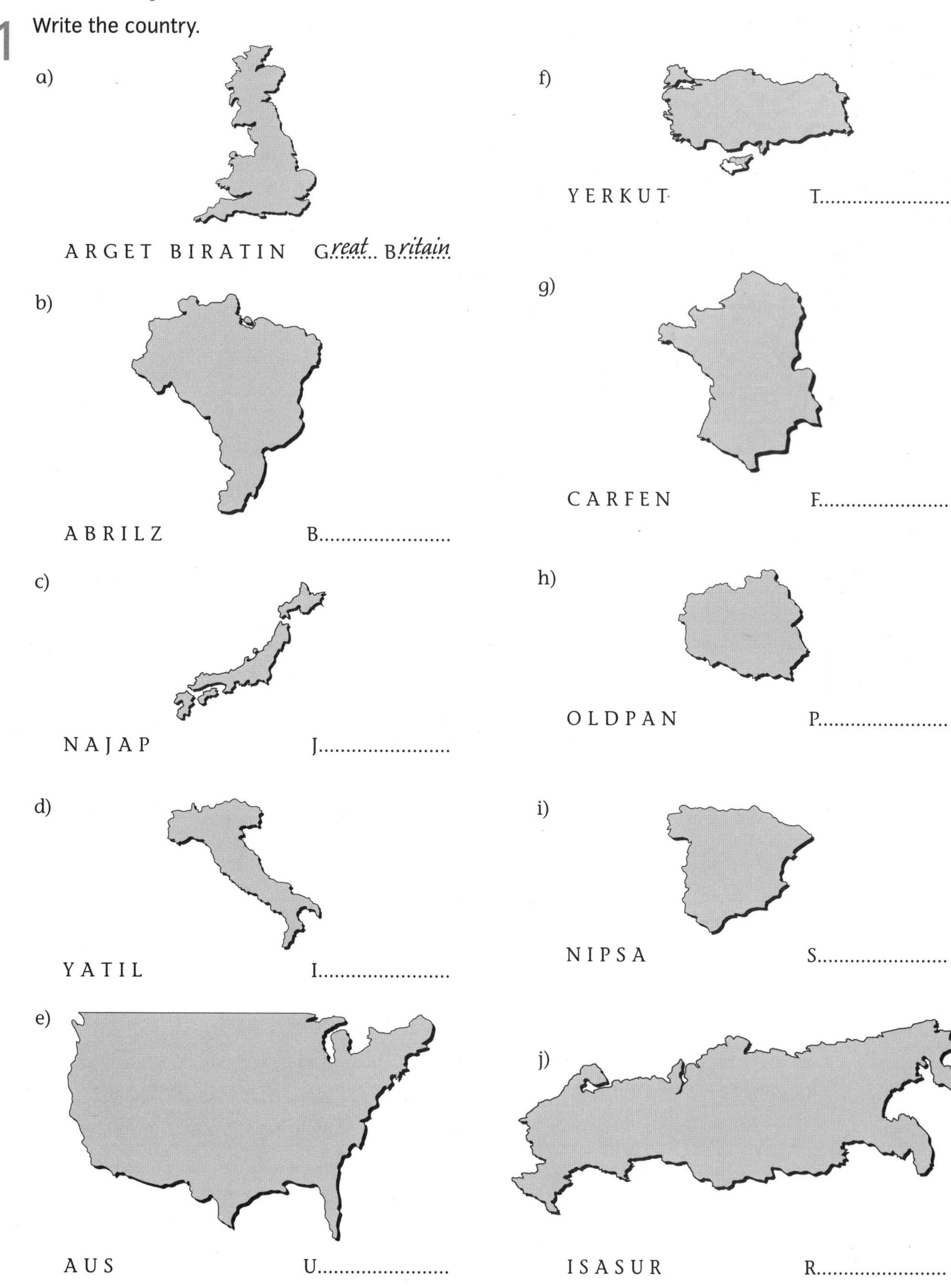

a) ARGET BIRATIN G*reat* B*ritain*

b) ABRILZ B........................

c) NAJAP J........................

d) YATIL I........................

e) AUS U........................

f) YERKUT T........................

g) CARFEN F........................

h) OLDPAN P........................

i) NIPSA S........................

j) ISASUR R........................

be with *I* and *you*

2 **a)** Put the words in order.

Adam: name's / Hello. / Adam / My / .
1 *Hello. My name's Adam.*
Francesca: Francesca. / I'm / you / Nice / to meet
2 *I'm* ....
Adam: are / from / ? / you / Where
3 .... ?
Francesca: Italy / from / I'm / .
4 ....
Adam: Rome / you / Are / from / ?
5 .... ?
Francesca: I'm / Milan / No, / from / .
6 ....
Francesca: you / student / a / Are / ?
7 .... ?
Adam: I'm / teacher / No, / your / .
8 ....

b) Listen and check.

Negatives

3 Make the sentences negative.

a) I'm from the United States.
I'm not from the United States.
b) You're from London.
....
c) You're a teacher.
....
d) I'm a teacher.
....
e) I'm from a big country.
....
f) You're from Russia.
....

Nationalities

4 **a)** Complete the sentences.

1 He's from Britain. He's *British* .
2 She's from the United States. She's ....
3 He's from Japan. He's ....
4 She's from France. She's ....
5 He's from Italy. He's ....
6 She's from Turkey. She's ....
7 She's from Russia. She's ....
8 He's from Spain. He's ....

b) Listen and check.

is/are/am

5 Write *am*, *are* or *is*.

a) How old *is* Ben?
b) .... I late?
c) .... your name Angela Zeller?
d) .... you from Japan?
e) Where .... I?
f) .... you married?
g) Where .... she from?
h) .... Carmen from Spain?

Questions

6 Make these sentences questions.

a) James is married.
Is James married?
b) You're from Australia.
....
c) Budapest is in Hungary.
....
d) You are 18.
....
e) Your name is Claudia.
....
f) He's French.
....
g) It's a Japanese car.
....
h) Edinburgh is the capital of Scotland.
....

Numbers 21–100

7 Underline the correct answer.

a) 11 + 11	= twelve	twenty-two	thirty-two
b) 86 – 63	= twenty-three	thirty-three	forty-three
c) 8 x 8	= forty-eight	fifty-six	sixty-four
d) 100 – 11	= seventy-nine	eighty-nine	ninety-nine
e) 9 x 3	= seventeen	twenty-seven	thirty-seven
f) 36 + 22	= fifty-two	fifty-six	fifty-eight
g) 13 x 6	= seventy-two	seventy-eight	eighty-four
h) 30 x 3	= sixty	eighty	ninety

Improve your writing

Writing about yourself

8 **a)** Read about Nicola. Fill the gaps with one word from the box.

~~is~~ single My from Please 'm email student

Hi!
Send Now | Send Later | Save as Draft | Add Attachments | Signature | Options
Subject: Hi!
Attachments: none
Default Font | Text Size

Hi!
My name (1) ...*is*... Nicola. (2) ....
surname is Harris. I (3) .... 20.
I'm (4) .... Manchester, in England. I'm a
(5) .... at Manchester University. My
(6) .... address is nicola@surfer.net I'm
(7) .... !
(8) .... write to me!!

b) Write an email about yourself.

Pronunciation

9 Listen and say these words and phrases.

a) he
b) he's
c) she
d) she's
e) meet
f) nice to meet you
g) please
h) three
i) see
j) see you later

Ages

10

Ricky Wood
Sydney, Australia
26

Jarek Zmuda
Warsaw, Poland
20

Çansel Sükür
Ankara, Turkey
17

Betty Fernandes
São Paulo, Brazil
41

a) Write the answers.

Ricky

1 What's his surname?
His surname is Wood.
2 Where is he from?
....
3 How old is he?
....

b) Listen and check.

c) Write the questions

Çansel

1 *What's her surname?*
Her surname is Sükür.
2 .... ?
She's from Ankara, Turkey.
3 .... ?
She's 17.

d) Listen and check.

e) Write questions and answers.

Jarek

1 *How old is he?*
He's 20.
2 What's his surname?
....
3 .... ?
He's from Warsaw, Poland.

f) Listen and check.

g) Write questions and answers.

Betty

1 How old is she?
....
2 .... ?
Her surname is Fernandes.
3 Where's she from?
....

h) Listen and check.

Capital letters (2)

11

> **We use capital letters ...** LOOK!
> with towns/cities
> *London, Istanbul, Rio de Janeiro*
> with countries
> *Poland, United States, Thailand*
> with nationalities
> *English, Brazilian, Korean*

Write the sentences with capital letters.

a) béatrice dalle is a french actress.
Béatrice Dalle is a French actress.
b) warsaw is the capital city of poland.
....
c) where is virginia from? i think she's argentinian.
....
d) osaka is a big city in japan.
....
e) i'm 21 and i'm russian.
....

Question words

12 Complete the questions with words from the box.

Where	How	~~What~~	Where	How	What	How	What

a) *What's* her job? — She's a teacher.
b) .... are you? — Fine, thank you. And you?
c) .... 's your first name? — Rita.
d) .... is Boris from? — I think he's from Mexico.
e) .... old is he? — I don't know.
f) .... 's your phone number? — 0207 737 7601
g) .... do you spell that? — M-A-R-T-I-N
h) .... 's Santiago? — In Chile.

Listen and read

Where in the world ...?

13 Listen and read about these places.

- **What is Yale and where is it?**
  Yale is a university in the United States of America – the USA. It's in New Haven, Connecticut.
- **What are the UK and the UAE?**
  The UK is the United Kingdom – England, Scotland Wales and Northern Ireland. London is the capital city of the United Kingdom. The UAE is the United Arab Emirates – seven countries in the Persian Gulf. The capital is Abu Dhabi.
- **What is Machu Picchu and where is it?**
  Machu Picchu is an old city in the Urabamba Valley in Peru, in South America.
- **Where is New South Wales? Is it in Wales?**
  No! New South Wales isn't in Wales ... and it isn't in the United Kingdom. It's in Australia ... the capital is Sydney.
- **Where is the Taj Mahal? How old is it?**
  The Taj Mahal is in Agra, a city in India. It's about 400 years old.

module 3

Vocabulary: nouns

1 Write the words.

a) a man........... b) a .... c) a .... d) a ....

e) a .... f) a .... g) a ....

Plural nouns

2 Write the plurals.

a) taxi	taxis	e) city	....
b) bus	....	f) man	....
c) child	....	g) woman	....
d) person	....	h) country	....

be: plural

3 Complete the sentences with *is* or *are*.

a) Glasgow and Edinburgh ....are..... cities in Scotland.
b) .... your name Thomas?
c) Her children .... ten and six years old.
d) New Delhi .... the capital of India.
e) Taxis .... expensive in my city.
f) Where .... your car?

Opposites

4 **a)** Complete the sentences with the opposite adjective.

1 Is the shop expensive?
– No, it's *cheap*...... .
2 Are you hot?
– No, I'm ....
3 Is Ali from a cold country?
– No, he's from a .... country.
4 Is your hotel big?
– No, it's ....
5 Are they small houses?
– No, they're ....
6 Is it a cheap holiday?
– No, it's ....

b) Listen and say the answers.

be with *we* and *they*

5 Complete the gaps with *we*, *they*, *are* or *aren't*.

a) Their names ....*are*..... Peter and Lynn. ....*They*.... 're from Australia.
b) Mr and Mrs Palmer .... in Room 838 – .... 're in Room 836.
c) ' .... you from the United States?'
'No, ... 're from Canada.'
d) No, we .... happy with our hotel: it's very cold, and it's expensive.
e) Eva and I .... Czech – .... 're from Prague.
f) Buses .... expensive in my city: .... 're very cheap.
g) Córdoba and Mendoza .... big cities in Argentina.
h) 'Is your hotel nice?'
'Yes, ... 're very happy with it.'

we're/they're/our/their

6 **a)** Match the questions and answers.

1	Where are you from?	a)	It's here.
2	What's our room number?	b)	Jim and Sam.
3	What are their names?	c)	We're at the hotel.
4	Where are the children?	d)	They're at school.
5	Where are you?	e)	323.
6	Where's our taxi?	f)	We're from Germany.

b) Listen and check.

Spelling

7 Tick (✓) the correct words and cross (✗) the incorrect words. Write the correct version next to the incorrect words.

1	city	.....✓.....	....
2	contry	.....✗.....	*country*
3	numbre	....	....
4	small	....	....
5	citys	....	....
6	people	....	....
7	espensive	....	....
8	water	....	....
9	beautifull	....	....
10	childern	....	....
11	marryed	....	....
12	fruit	....	....

Food and drink vocabulary

8 Find a word for food and drink in each line of letters. Underline the word.

1	D	G	F	C	R	I	C	E	G	T	U	Y
2	B	T	T	E	L	E	G	G	S	I	W	N
3	S	C	H	E	E	S	E	A	E	T	P	Y
4	T	E	N	L	P	E	S	R	M	E	A	T
5	A	E	V	E	G	E	T	A	B	L	E	S
6	N	M	D	F	T	B	R	E	A	D	H	T
7	S	N	B	T	F	I	S	H	B	R	S	J
8	A	C	O	F	F	E	E	C	R	I	G	O
9	N	R	G	E	L	R	W	M	I	L	K	W
10	Y	S	H	G	H	W	A	T	E	R	H	T
11	M	N	S	G	T	S	I	P	A	S	T	A
12	I	I	A	D	F	R	U	I	T	P	I	W

this/that/these/those

9 Underline the correct word.

a) 'Is *this/these* your pen?'
b) Are *that/those* people from Japan?
c) 'Who's *that/those?*' 'My teacher.'
d) 'What are *that/those?*' 'I don't know!'
e) 'Is *this/these* your car?' 'Yes, it is.'
f) 'Who are *that/those* children over there?'
g) 'Is *that/those* hotel expensive?' 'Yes, it is!'

Prepositions

10 Write the preposition.

LOOK!

at + school, university
*Nicola is a student **at** Manchester University.*

from + city/country
*She's **from** England.*

in + city/country
*Dublin is **in** Ireland.*

on
*They're **on** holiday.*

a) Florence and her husband are French – they're *from*..... Paris.
b) We're .... holiday in Spain.
c) The children aren't here; they're .... school.
d) Are the hotels expensive .... your country?
e) Is New Mexico .... the United States?
f) 'Where is George .... ?' 'Greece.'
g) 'Where's Red Square?' 'It's .... Moscow.'

Pronunciation

11 Listen and say these words and phrases.

a) bus
b) classroom
c) address
d) small
e) friends
f) his friends
g) cheese
h) eggs
i) cities
j) buses
k) those shops
l) these houses

Listen and read

Eating and drinking around the world

12 Listen and read about these people's favourite food and drink.

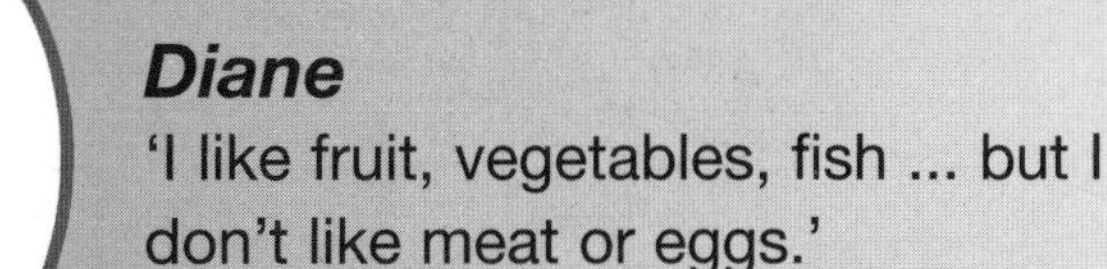

Diane
'I like fruit, vegetables, fish ... but I don't like meat or eggs.'

Ross
'My favourite food is pasta ... I like lasagne, spaghetti, tagliatelle ... No, I'm not Italian! I'm from Scotland!'

Sachiko
'My favourite food is sushi – it's rice with fish. It's from Japan – my country.'

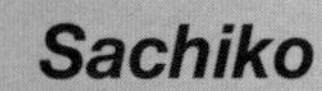

Luis
'I'm from Spain. I like Manchego – it's from La Mancha, in Spain. It's my favourite cheese.'

Barbara and Tony
'We're on holiday in Turkey ... and we like the food. Our favourite Turkish food is shish kebap – meat with rice – it's very good!'

Improve your writing

A postcard

13

Use words and phrases in the box to write the postcard.

~~everybody~~	are very good	We're here	expensive
in a hotel	See you	How	beautiful

Hello (a) *everybody* !!
(b) .... are you?
(c) .... in Greece on holiday.
We're (d) .... - its name is the Miramar. It's (e) .... ! - #250 a day!
We're at the beach now! It's (f) .... ! The weather and the food (g) ....
(h) .... soon!

Christopher, Martha and the children
Flat D, 128 Canterbury Road
Ashford,
Kent AS9 GHS
England

Vocabulary: places in a town

1 Write the missing letters.

a) BANK

b) B _ S S _ _ P

c) R _ S T _ _ R _ _ T

d) _ T _ T _ _ N

e) _ A _ P _ _ K

f) S _ P _ R _ _ _ K _ T

g) _ Q _ A _ E

Prepositions

2 **a)** Underline the correct word(s) and phrases.

1 The bank's *in/on* the square.
2 'Where's the station?' 'It's *in/on* the left.'
3 The restaurant's on *right/the right*.
4 Is your hotel near *of the station/the station*?
5 The cinema is on the left *of the restaurant/the restaurant*.
6 Is the hotel *in/at* Station Road?

b) Listen and check.

there is/there are

3 **a)** Read the information about Crowley and complete the sentences with *there's* or *there are*.

Crowley Town Guide

Hotel:	Hotel Europe (**), Park Street
Restaurants:	Il Buongustaio (Italian), Church Street
	Jasmine Peking (Chinese), St. Michael's Street
	The Crab & Lobster (Fish), Marton Street
Cafés:	The Pear Tree, Church Street
	Frederick's, Bridge Street
	Market Café, Market Square
Supermarket:	Tesco, Marton Road
Cinema:	Odeon, Church Street
Car Parks:	St. Michael's Street, Camley Road.
Banks:	NatWest / Barclays, Market Square
Post Office:	Park Street

** = two star

1 *There's* a hotel in Crowley.
2 .... three restaurants.
3 .... an Italian restaurant.
4 .... three cafés.
5 .... a supermarket in Marton Road.
6 .... a cinema in Church Street.
7 .... two car parks.
8 .... two banks in Market Square: *NatWest* and *Barclays*.
9 .... a post office in Park Street.

b) Listen and check.

Negative sentences

4 **a)** Write negative sentences about Crowley.

1 (*a ***** hotel*)
There isn't a 5-star hotel.
2 (*any Indian restaurants*)
....
3 (*a railway station*)
....
4 (*any Internet cafés*)
....
5 (*a library*)
....
6 (*any beaches*)
....

b) Listen and repeat the sentences.

Questions

5 **a)** Write questions about Crowley.

1 (*a park*)
Is there a park?
2 (*any good shops*)
.... ?
3 (*a university*)
.... ?
4 (*a bus station*)
.... ?
5 (*any interesting bars*)
.... ?
6 (*a cinema*)
.... ?

b) Listen and repeat the answers.

All forms

6 Match the two halves to make six sentences.

a) There are ...   1 ... any French students in my class.
b) There's a ...   2 ... any good shops near here?
c) There isn't ...   3 ... good supermarket in this street.
d) There aren't ...   4 ... a university in your town?
e) Is there ...   5 ... a lot of students in my city.
f) Are there ...   6 ... a restaurant at the station.

some, *any* and *a*

7 Complete the sentences with *some*, *any* or *a*.

a) There's .....a..... beautiful park near my house.
b) There are .... good restaurants in the Market Square.
c) Are there .... small children in your family?
d) Is there .... cinema in this town?
e) There aren't .... famous people in my family.
f) There isn't .... car park at the university.
g) There's .... bus stop in Hope Street.
h) There are .... American students at my university.

Common adjectives

8 Write the adjective.

a) I like Paris ... it's a very b e a u t i f u l city.
b) 'Is your book i _ _ _ _ _ _ _ _ _ _ _?' 'Yes ... it's very good.'

c) There's a nice park near here ... it's q _ _ _ _ .
d) Sophie Marceau is a f _ _ _ _ _ actress from France.
e) This is a very b _ _ _ street: there are always a lot of cars.

f) It's a very s _ _ _ _ hotel – there are only ten rooms.
g) There are a lot of n _ _ _ people in my school.

Listen and read

9 **a)** Listen to and read the text about *The World Showcase*.

The World Showcase

The World Showcase **is in DisneyWorld in Florida, USA. There are eleven pavilions at the beautiful *World Showcase Lagoon* – and all the pavilions are about a different country in the world.**

In the Chinese pavilion, there are two Chinese restaurants. In the Moroccan pavilion, there's a real Moroccan market.
For France, there's the Eiffel Tower (a small one!) and there's a cinema.

In the Italian pavilion, there's an Italian restaurant – *Alfredo's* – with real Italian pasta!

And in the United Kingdom pavilion, there's a pub – *The Rose and Crown* – with English food and drinks.

In the Japanese pavilion there's a Japanese garden, and a big Japanese store* – *Mitsukoshi*.

* *store* in American English = *shop* in British English

b) Answer these questions about *The World Showcase*.

1 Where are the Chinese restaurants?
In the Chinese pavilion.

2 Where is *Alfredo's* restaurant?
....

3 Where is the cinema?
....

4 Where is *The Rose and Crown* pub?
....

5 Where is the *Mitsukoshi* store?
....

6 Where is the market?
....

Improve your writing

Capital letters (revision)

10

LOOK!

We use capital letters ...

with names	*Frederick Smith*
at the beginning of a sentence	*Hello. My name's ...*
with *I*	*Do I know you?*

We also use capital letters ...:

with countries	*Turkey*	*Italy*	*Argentina*
with languages	*Arabic*	*Spanish*	*Japanese*
with nationalities	*American*	*Brazilian*	*Australian*
with towns and cities	*New York*	*Rome*	*Cairo*

Write the capital letters.

a) german is an official language in austria and switzerland.
German is an official language in Austria and Switzerland.

b) 'is andrea bocelli spanish?' 'no, he's italian.'

....

....

c) london is the capital city of england. there's also a london in Canada and two in the united states!!

....

....

d) there are two official languages in canada – french and english.

....

....

e) spanish is the official language in argentina, chile and uruguay – but in brazil the official language is portuguese.

....

....

is or *are*?

11 **a)** Complete the sentences with *is* or *are*.

1 ...*Is*.... there a hotel near here?
2 There .... two banks in Station Road.
3 There .... some very interesting places to visit.
4 Roseville .... a small town in the USA.
5 .... there any nice restaurants here?
6 There .... a big park in the town centre.

b) Listen and check.

Pronunciation

12 Listen and say these words and phrases.

a) famous
b) small
c) beautiful
d) busy
e) quiet

f) a famous city
g) a small café
h) a beautiful beach
i) a busy restaurant
j) a quiet town

Family vocabulary

1 Marta is from Mexico. This is her family.

daughter children ~~husband~~ son wife

a) Write the correct word from the box.

1 Antonio is Marta's *husband* .
2 Marta is Antonio's ....
3 They have two .... – Javier and Gloria.
4 Gloria is their ....
5 Their .... 's name is Javier.

b) Listen and check.

c) Write the correct word from the box.

parents ~~brother~~ father mother sister

6 Javier is Gloria's *brother* .
7 Gloria is Javier's ....
8 Antonio and Marta are Javier and Gloria's ....
9 Marta is their ....
10 Antonio is their ....

d) Listen and check.

e) Write the correct word from the box.

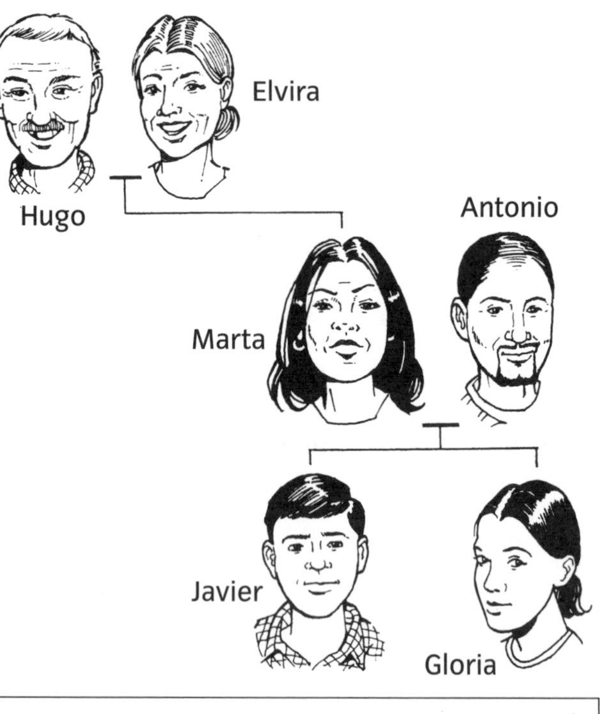

grandson granddaughter ~~grandparents~~ grandfather grandmother grandchildren

11 Hugo and Elvira are Gloria and Javier's *grandparents* .
12 Hugo is their ....
13 Elvira is their ....
14 Gloria and Javier are Hugo and Elvira's ....
15 Gloria is their ....
16 Javier is their ....

f) Listen and check.

Possessive 's

2 Write 's in the correct place.

a) Is that Paul's mother?
b) What's your sister name?
c) John brother is a footballer.
d) There's a party at Frank house!
e) 'Is this your book?' 'No, it's Barbara.'
f) Jackie is Catherine sister.
g) Our dog name is Max.

's = *is* or possessive?

3 Write *possessive* or *is* for each sentence below.

a) My father's name is Frederick. 's = possessive
b) What's her name? 's = is
c) He's from Scotland. 's = ...
d) Ana's children are at school. 's = ...
e) Claire's husband is Spanish. 's = ...
f) His name's Tony. 's = ...
g) Michael's parents are on holiday. 's = ...
h) Pablo's a footballer from Chile. 's = ...

Verbs

4 Write the verb in the circle.

a) (study) French / at university / a lot
b) ( ) in a big city / with your family / in Poland
c) ( ) for an international company / with children / in the centre of town
d) ( ) three children / a good job / a lot of friends

Present Simple

Negative

5 Write *don't* in the correct place to make negative sentences.

a) We don't have an expensive car.
b) I study French.
c) I work in the centre of town.
d) I have a brother.
e) We live in Poland.
f) Our children drink tea.

Questions

6 **a)** Write the questions for these answers.

1 (live/house/flat)
Do you live in a house or a flat?
I live in a flat.

2 (study/German)
.... ?
No, I don't. I study English!

3 (have/any children)
.... ?
Yes, two. Their names are Tom and Anna.

4 (live/town/city)
.... ?
I live in Fermo, it's a town in Italy.

5 (have/any pets)
.... ?
No. I don't like animals.

6 (have/any brothers and sisters)
.... ?
Yes, one brother. His name's Mark.

b) Listen and check. Repeat the questions.

Short answers

7 **a)** Write the short answers.

1 Do you live in a house? ✓ *Yes, I do.*
2 Do you study Japanese? ✗ *No, I don't.*
3 Do you have any sisters? ✓ ....
4 Do you live in America? ✗ ....
5 Do you like dogs? ✓ ....
6 Do you have a dog? ✗ ....

b) Listen and check. Repeat the answers.

Question words: *How*, *What*, *Where*, *Who*

8 Complete the questions with the correct question words: *how*, *what*, *where* or *who*.

a) *What* are their names? Tim and Helen.
b) .... do you live? In Moscow.
c) .... old is your brother? He's 24.
d) .... do you live with? With my husband.
e) .... are your parents? They're fine.
f) .... are your parents? They're in the United States

Personal possessions

9 Write the missing letters.

a) B *I* C *Y* C L *E*
b) M _ N _ Y
c) M O B _ L _ _ _ O N _
d) _ A T _ _
e) M _ _ A _ I _ E
f) G _ _ S _ _ S
g) R _ D _ _
h) P _ R _ E
i) W _ L _ E _
j) _ A _ _ R _
k) C _ _ D _ T _ A R _

Improve your writing

Writing about your family

10

a) Underline the correct phrase about Donna's family.

1 My *name's/names* Donna.
2 I live *at/with* my parents in a nice flat in Dublin, Ireland.
3 I *don't/'m not* have a big family: just Mum, Dad, me and *my/your* brother.
4 My parents' names *is/are* Declan and Rosemary.
5 My *brother/brother's* name is Ciaran.
6 We also have two cats: *his/their* names are Benny and Bjorn.
7 I have three *grandfathers/grandparents*.
8 My grandmother's *name/names* is Iris, and *she is/they are* 71 years old.

b) Write some sentences about **your** family.

Prepositions

11

Use a preposition from the box to complete the sentences.

~~in~~ with in in for with with in

a) There's a bank ....*in*.... the centre of the city.
b) 'Where's Rosario?' 'It's .... Argentina.'
c) I don't live .... my family – I live alone.
d) I like my job – I work .... computers.
e) Do you work .... a big company?
f) It's a very nice house .... a big garden.
g) I don't live .... a flat. I live .... a house.

Articles

12

Write *a* in the correct place.

Louise

a) 'I live in *a* flat in Manchester.'
b) 'I work for German bank.'

Gabor

c) 'I'm medical student.'
d) 'There are lot of people in my flat!'

Carolina

e) 'We're big family.'
f) 'I have four brothers and sister.'
g) 'We have very big house.'

Pronunciation

13

Listen and say these words, phrases and sentences.

a) with
b) brother
c) father
d) mother
e) this
f) these
g) This is my mother.
h) with my mother and father
i) I'm with my brother.
j) This is my father.
k) What's this?
l) How much are these?

Listen and read

14 **a)** Listen to and read the text.

Facts and Figures

- **1,600,000 people in India work for the Indian Railway Company – that's 1.8% of the country's population!!**
- **About 650,000 students in the UK study foreign languages at school – 52% study French; 21% study German; 7% study Spanish and 20% study other languages.**
- **32 million people live in the South American republic of Argentina. About 11 million live in or near the capital city, Buenos Aires – that's about 34% of the population.**
- **Around the world, about 500 million homes have a television. 89% of homes in the United States have a video recorder: but it's only 13% in China!**

b) Complete these sentences with the correct numbers.

1 .... % of homes in China have a video recorder.
2 .... million people live in or near Argentina's capital city.
3 .... % of India's population work for the Indian Railway Company.
4 .... million homes in the world have a television.
5 The population of Argentina is .... million.
6 .... % of foreign language students in schools in the UK study Spanish.

module 6

Vocabulary: likes and dislikes

1

I hate	I don't like	love	... is okay	~~I like~~

a) Write sentences about Shirley.

Chinese food

1 *'I like Chinese food.'*...

Robbie Williams

2 '..'

cooking

3 '..'

classical music

4 '..'

football

5 '..'

b) Listen and check.

Object pronouns

2 Replace the word or phrase in **bold** with a pronoun from the box.

~~them~~	it	it	him	them	her	it

a) 'Do you like cats?'
'Yes, I love ~~cats~~.'
them

b) 'Do you like Mexican food?'
'Yes, I love **Mexican food**.'
....

c) 'Do you like Céline Dion?'
'Yes, I love **Céline Dion**.'
....

d) Robbie Williams is awful!
I hate **Robbie Williams**!
....

e) 'Do you like tea?'
'Yes, I love **tea**.'
....

f) Small dogs ... I hate **small dogs**!!
....

g) 'Do you play football?'
'No, but I watch **football** on TV.'
....

Vocabulary: useful nouns

3 Write the words.

a) People read ...	K O B O S	b*ooks*...........
	P R E S S E P A W N	n *ewspapers*
b) People play ...	M E G A S	g..................
	F A T L O B O L	f..................
c) People watch ...	T E N I V O I L E S	t..................
	C O R N O S T A	c..................
d) People use them at home and at work	R E M O P C U T S	c..................
	T E R I N N E T	i..................
e) People drink	O F F E C E	c..................
	A T E	t..................
f) a big shop	M U P E T K R A R S E	s..................

Present Simple: *he* and *she*

4 Write the *he* or *she* form of the verb.

a) My father really ...*likes*... football. (*like*)
b) Patricia .... the Internet at work. (*use*)
c) Our daughter .... a lot of television. (*watch*)
d) Dario .... for an international company. (*work*)
e) My father .... the newspaper at work. (*read*)
f) Danielle is a teacher: she .... French. (*teach*)
g) My friend Bob .... in the United States. (*live*)
h) David is a footballer: he .... for Manchester United. (*play*)
i) Jackie .... three brothers and three sisters. (*have*)

Pronunciation

5 Listen and say these words, phrases and sentences.

a) read	g) reads the newspaper
b) reads	h) He reads the newspaper.
c) like	i) she likes
d) likes	j) She likes shopping.
e) work	k) she works
f) works	l) She works in a bank.

Present Simple

Questions

6 Look at the picture of Tina and Tony and read their answers to the questions.

	Tina	Tony
Food and drink Do you … eat meat? drink a lot of coffee?	 No, I'm a vegetarian. No.	 Yes … I love burgers!! Yes.
Music Do you … like rock music? like dancing?	 No, I hate it! Yes.	 Yes. No.
Languages Do you … study a foreign language? speak French?	 Yes. Yes.	 No … I only speak English. No.
Free time Do you … play a sport? like computer games?	 Yes, I play tennis. No.	 No. Yes, I love them!!

a) Write questions and answers about Tina and Tony, as in the example.

1 *(eat meat)*
Does Tina eat meat? No, she doesn't.
Does Tony eat meat? Yes, he does.

2 *(drink a lot of coffee)*
……………………………………
……………………………………

3 *(like rock music)*
……………………………………
……………………………………

4 *(like dancing)*
……………………………………
……………………………………

5 *(study a foreign language)*
……………………………………
……………………………………

6 *(speak French)*
……………………………………
……………………………………

7 *(play a sport)*
……………………………………
……………………………………

8 *(like computer games)*
……………………………………
……………………………………

b) Listen and check.

Negative

7 Make these sentences negative.

a) My dog likes cats.
My dog doesn't like cats.

b) Paul teaches English.
....

c) Carla lives with her parents.
....

d) My father likes rock music.
....

e) Sam plays tennis.
....

f) Olga works for a British company.
....

g) Brian speaks Japanese.
....

All forms

8 Underline the correct verb form.

a) Michael *come/comes* from Canada.
b) Mary *work/works* for a German bank, but she doesn't *speak/speaks* German at work – she *speak/speaks* English all the time!
c) 'Does Luis *play/plays* basketball?'
'No, he *doesn't/don't*. But he *watch/watches* it on TV.
d) Jane *doesn't/don't* eat meat or fish, but she *eat/eats* eggs.
e) Maggie *teach/teaches* French in a language school, but she doesn't *like/likes* her job.
f) Johnny *like/likes* rock music, but he *doesn't/don't* like rap music and he *hate/hates* jazz!
g) '*Do/Does* your mother like shopping?'
'Yes, she *does/do*. She *love/loves* it!'

Improve your writing

Using pronouns

9 **a)** Complete the text using words from the box.

live Her ~~She~~ city He's
They their He

A couple

Agnes is a singer. [1] *She* is from Szeged, a [2]................. in the south of Hungary. [3]................. husband's name is Roberto. [4]................. a singer, too. [5]................. is Italian. They now [6]................. in Budapest, the capital city of Hungary. [7]................. don't have any children, but they have two cats: [8]................. names are Brahms and Liszt.

b) Write a similar paragraph about a couple you know – famous or not!

Listen and read

Famous couples

10 a) Listen to and read the texts about two famous couples.

Will Smith and Jada Pinkett Smith

Will Smith is an American actor and rap singer from Philadelphia, USA. He is in the TV series *Fresh Prince of Bel Air* and in the films *Men in Black* (1996) and *Independence Day* (1997). His wife is actress Jada Pinkett Smith. She is in *The Nutty Professor* with Eddie Murphy and in the film *Scream II*. They have two children – Jaden and Willow – and they live in Los Angeles.

Iman and David Bowie

Iman – her full name is Iman Abdulmajid – is 47 years old and she comes from Somalia in Africa. She is a supermodel, an actress and an international businesswoman. She is married to British rock star and actor David Bowie (real name David Robert Jones). They both have one child from other marriages, and now they have a daughter, Alexandra Zahra Jones. They live in New York.

b) Write answers to the questions about Will Smith and Jada Pinkett Smith.

1 Does Will Smith appear in the film *Men in Black*?
Yes, he does.

2 Where is he from?
....

3 What is his wife's name?
....

4 What are their children's names?
....

5 Where do Will and Jada live now?
....

c) Listen and check.

d) Write questions for the answers about Iman and David Bowie.

1 *How old is Iman?*
She's 47 years old.

2 ....
She's from Somalia.

3 ....
Yes, she is – to David Bowie.

4 ....
Yes – they have one daughter.

5 ....
They live in New York.

e) Listen and check.

module 7

Daily routines

1 **a)** Complete the text using words from the box

~~get up~~ get have sleep start finish have go go have

My name's Margaret Beech. I'm a journalist.

I [1]...*get up*.. early, at quarter to six, and [2]............. to work at about half past six. I [3]............. breakfast in a café near my office, and [4]............. work at half past seven. I don't [5]............. a big lunch, just a sandwich and a coffee. I usually [6]............. work at about six o'clock. I [7]............. home at seven, then I [8]............. dinner with my husband - he loves cooking! After dinner we usually watch TV, then I [9]............. to bed early, at about ten o'clock, and [10]............. for seven or eight hours.

b) Listen and check.

Present Simple

Questions

2 **a)** Look at the answers and write questions about Margaret's daily routine.

1 What time .*does she get up*.. ?
At quarter to six.
2 When .... work?
At about half past six.
3 Where .... breakfast?
In a café near her office.
4 What time .... work?
At half past seven.
5 .... a big lunch?
No, she doesn't.
6 When .... work?
At about six o'clock.
7 What time .... home?
At about seven in the evening.
8 .... bed early?
Yes, she does.

b) Listen and check. Practise saying the questions.

All forms

3 **a)** (Circle) the correct answer.

1 What time (do)/does you (get)/gets up in the morning?
2 My husband *don't/doesn't* usually *start/starts* work before nine.
3 *Do/Does* your brother *work/works* on Saturdays?
4 My parents *finish/finishes* work at about five.
5 When *do/does* you *have/has* lunch?
6 After work I *don't/doesn't* usually *go/goes* home.
7 *Do/Does* Antonio *have/has* dinner at home every night?
8 My cat usually *sleep/sleeps* in my bedroom!

b) Listen and check.

Vocabulary: days of the week

4 Write the days of the week. Number them in the correct order.

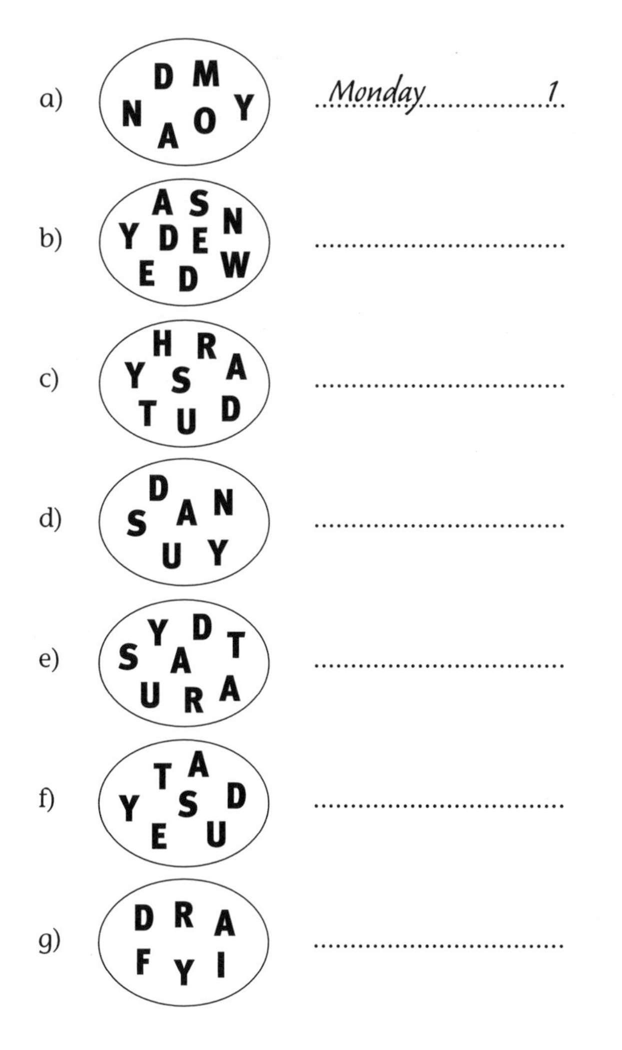

Adverbs of frequency

5 **a)** Complete these adverbs of frequency.

1 U S U A L L Y
2 A _ _ A _ S
3 N _ _ _ R
4 N _ T U _ _ A _ L _
5 S _ M _ T _ _ E _

b) Put the words from **a** in the correct place on the line.

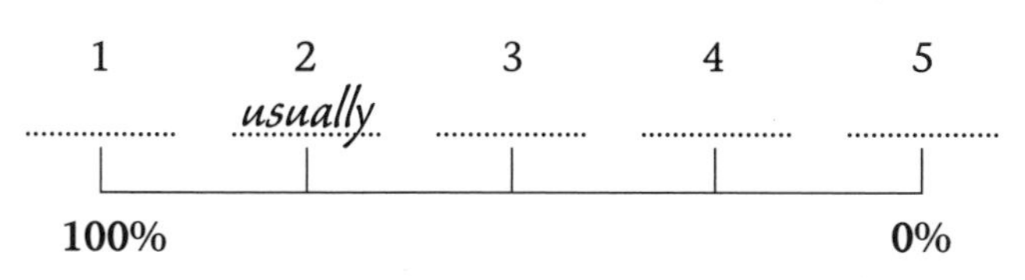

Word order with adverbs

6 **a)** Put the adverbs of frequency in the correct place in the sentences below.

1 I sometimes get up early. (sometimes)
2 I don't play tennis at the weekend. (usually)
3 My brother and I play football at the weekend. (always)

4 Shops in our town open at night. (sometimes)

5 Barbara doesn't work on Mondays. (usually)
6 I listen to music when I get home. (usually)
7 Children in Britain go to school on Sundays. (never)
8 We go to work by train. (always)

b) Listen and check.

Verbs and nouns

7 Choose the correct verb from the box.

~~stay~~ meet listen to read watch go to clean go do

a) ....*stay*.... in
b) .... the house
c) .... friends
d) .... { the cinema / the supermarket / a club / a restaurant
e) .... your homework
f) .... { TV / sport
g) .... { a book / a newspaper
h) .... music
i) .... shopping

Time expressions

8 **a)** Complete the sentences with *in*, *on*, *at* or Ø (no preposition).

1 I don't go to work ......*on*...... Saturday.
2 What do you do .... the weekend?
3 My father plays tennis .... every Wednesday.
4 The concert is .... eight o'clock .... Monday evening.
5 Abdul usually does his homework .... the afternoon.
6 We usually go to the cinema .... every week.
7 I usually get up .... nine o'clock .... the morning.
8 Most people don't work .... night or .... Sundays.

b) Listen and check.

Telling the time

9 Write the times.

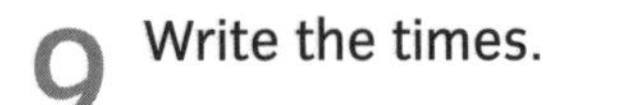

a) *five past eleven*........ b) .... c) .... d) ....

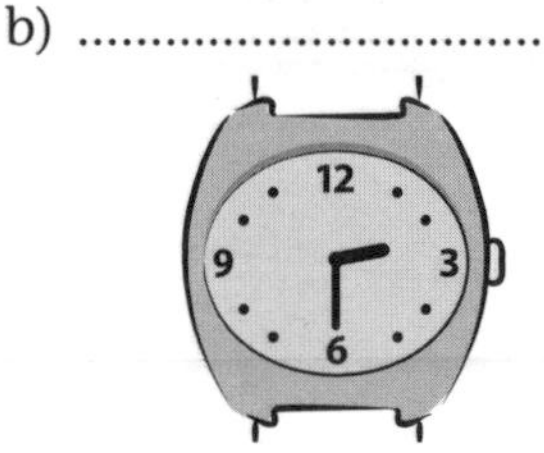

e) .... f) .... g) .... h) ....

Listen and read

Life in Britain today

10 **a)** Listen to and read the text about life in Britain today.

Life in Britain Today

Food
British people like good food, and more than half of them go to a restaurant every month. Fast food is also very popular – 30% of all adults have a burger every three months, but 46% have fish and chips!

Sport
British people don't do a lot of sport. Only 17% of people go swimming every week, 9% go cycling and 8% play golf – and only 6% of people play football (but 32% go to watch it).

Cinema and TV
Films are very popular in Britain, and about 60% of people between 15 and 24 go to the cinema every month. At home, men watch TV for about three hours every day – half an hour more than women.

Holidays
British people love going on holiday, and have 56 million holidays every year. Most of these holidays aren't in the UK – 27% are in Spain, 10% are in the USA, and 9% are in France. Maybe this is because the weather in Britain isn't very good!

b) Read the text again and underline the correct answers in the sentences below.

1 The favourite food in Britain is: a) *burgers* b) *fish and chips.*

2 17% of British people a) *go swimming* b) *play golf* c) *play football* every week.

3 British men watch about a) *2 hours* b) *3 hours* c) *4 hours* of TV every day.

4 Their favourite country for a holiday is a) *Spain* b) *France* c) *the USA.*

Improve your writing

Personal descriptions

11

name	Jacopo Barigazzi
city	Milan, Italy
age	28
job	computer engineer
in the week	Monday evening: have a violin lesson Thursday afternoon: play tennis with his brother
Friday evening	usually/have dinner in a restaurant sometimes/go to a club
weekend	always/get up late sometimes/go to a friend's house/afternoon

a) Look at the information about Jacopo and complete the paragraph.

Jacopo Barigazzi *lives in Milan*............ , in Italy. He's 28, and he's a .... On Monday evenings he .... , and on Thursday afternoons he .... On Friday evenings he usually .... , and he sometimes .... At the weekend he .... , and he .... afternoon.

b) Write a similar paragraph about a person you know.

Spelling

Double letters

12

Circle the word with the correct spelling.

a) footbal/football (circled)
b) realy/really
c) always/allways
d) usualy/usually
e) travel/travell
f) cooking/cookking
g) shoping/shopping
h) cigarete/cigarette
i) finish/finnish
j) cofee/coffee

Pronunciation

13

Listen and say these words, phrases and sentences.

a) work
b) word
c) first
d) Thursday
e) walk
f) sport
g) small
h) I walk to work.
i) Is she your daughter?
j) a small burger
k) She walks home.
l) Do you work on Thursdays?

module 8

Action verbs

1 Match the verbs to the pictures.

~~stand~~ walk swim ride talk sit run see hear play

a) *stand*..
f) ....
b) ....
g) .... a bicycle
c) ....
h) ....
d) .... the guitar
i) ....
e) ....
j) ....

can and *can't*

2 **a)** Complete the sentences with *can* or *can't*.

1 I *can*........ ride a bicycle, but I *can't*....... swim.
2 .... you play chess?
3 Margie's always late for work because she .... get up early.

4 .... your husband cook?
5 Their daughter's only six months old, so she .... talk or read.
6 .... you speak any foreign languages?
7 I'm sorry, I .... understand this sentence.
8 My sister .... play the violin brilliantly.

b)  Listen and check.

Short answers

3 **a)** Complete the answers.

1 Can you cook?
Yes, *I can*.
2 Can your parents speak English?
No, ...
3 Can Jim play football well?
No, ...
4 Can your daughter read and write?
Yes, ...
5 Can you swim?
No, ...
6 Can your son read music?
Yes, ...
7 Can your friends play tennis?
Yes, ...

b) Listen and check.

Vocabulary: parts of the body

4 Write the parts of the body.

a) *head*
b) ....
c) ....
d) ....
e) ....
f) ....
g) ....
h) ....
i) ....

Vocabulary: quantities

5 Complete the sentences with words from the box.

~~grams~~ days centimetres hours litres kilometres minutes metres kilos seconds

a) Can I have 300 *grams* of cheese, please?
b) In the Olympics, men run the 400 .... in about 45 ....
c) An average two-year-old boy is 91 .... tall.
d) Most people sleep for eight .... every night.
e) A new baby weighs about three or four ....
f) It's about 8,100 .... from Rome to Beijing.
g) There are 365 .... in a year.
h) We buy milk and water in ....
i) A football match is ninety .... long.

Questions

Question words

6 **a)** Look at an interview with Chad Martin, a famous Hollywood actor. Complete the questions with the words and phrases in the box.

~~What~~ Where Who Why How many When

1 ...*What*... 's the name of your new film?
2 .... is it in cinemas?
3 .... do people like your films?
4 .... 's your favourite actor?
5 .... 's your wife from?
6 .... houses do you have?

b) Match the questions with the answers.

A Three, I think ... no, four!
B I love Robert de Niro – he's great!
C It's called *Blood in the Afternoon.*
D She's from Palermo, in Italy.
E On Friday.
F Because they're fast and exciting, I think.

1 - C

c) Listen and check.

Forming questions

7 **a)** Write questions for the underlined words. Start each question with a question word from Exercise 6.

1 *How many people live in the UK?*
About 56 million people live in the UK.
2 ....
My brother lives in Egypt.
3 ....
Bogotá's the capital of Colombia.
4 ....
Elton John's my favourite singer.
5 ....
I study English because I want to get a good job.
6 ....
We usually go to the cinema on Tuesdays.
7 ....
Monica speaks four languages.

b) Listen and check.

Big numbers

8 **a)** Write the numbers.

1 10,000
ten thousand
2 3,000,000
....
3 2,500
....
4 365
....
5 100,000
....
6 700
....
7 9,999
....

b) Listen and check.

Listen and read

Living in the Antarctic

9 **a)** Listen to and read the following text.

Living *in the* Antarctic

'Hi, my name's Max Wright. I'm an engineer, and I live on the Scott Base in the Antarctic. It's *very* cold here, of course. At night the temperature can be -50 °C, but in the day it's only -20 °C!

Twelve people live here, and we're all from New Zealand. At the base there's a restaurant, a TV room, a small shop, and six bedrooms – two people sleep in each room. Most of our food comes from New Zealand, and we also eat fish from the sea.

We work from Monday to Friday, and sometimes Saturdays too. Every morning I go swimming in the sea (which is only 1 °C!), and in my free time I play volleyball or watch videos. I also love watching the animals and birds, especially the penguins – there are thousands of them here.

Yes, it's cold at Scott Base, but it's also a very beautiful place to live. I love it here.'

b) Read the text again and answer these questions.

1 What is Max's job?

....

2 What's the temperature at Scott Base in the day?

....

3 How many people live there?

....

4 What does Max do every morning?

....

5 What does he do in his free time?

....

6 Does he like living at Scott Base?

....

Spelling: 'silent' letters

10 **a)** Complete the words with the missing letters.

1 *w*rite
2 mount _ in
3 We _ nesday
4 int _ resting
5 veg _ tables
6 _ rong
7 forei _ n language
8 dau _ _ ter
9 lis _ en
10 g _ itar

b) We don't pronounce these letters. Listen and practise saying the words.

Pronunciation

Wh- questions

12 Listen and say these questions.

a) Who's your favourite actress?
b) Where do you work?
c) When do you go to bed?
d) Why do you study English?
e) What do you do in the evening?
f) How many people are there?

Improve your writing

Describing yourself

11 **a)** Read the paragraph about Corina and complete the text with phrases from the box.

~~My name's~~	write to me	I can	In my free time
I usually	I love	I live in	I also study

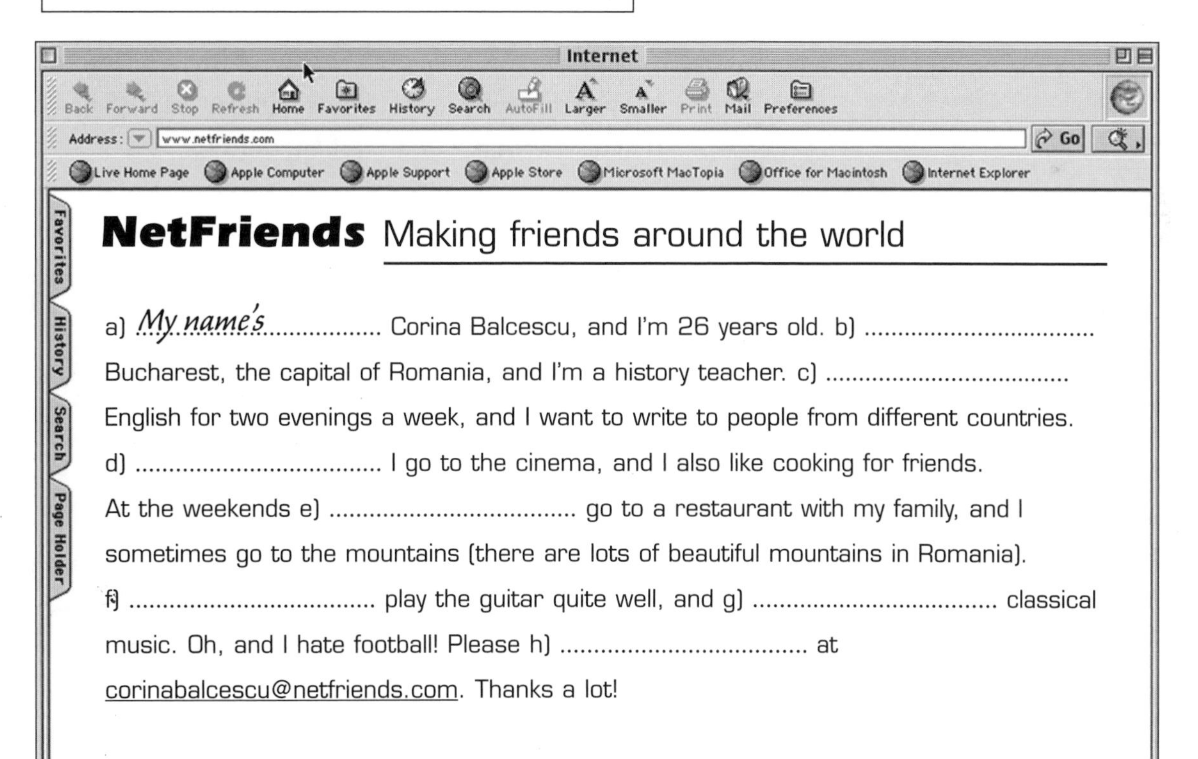

NetFriends Making friends around the world

a) *My name's*.................. Corina Balcescu, and I'm 26 years old. b) .... Bucharest, the capital of Romania, and I'm a history teacher. c) .... English for two evenings a week, and I want to write to people from different countries. d) .... I go to the cinema, and I also like cooking for friends. At the weekends e) .... go to a restaurant with my family, and I sometimes go to the mountains (there are lots of beautiful mountains in Romania). f) .... play the guitar quite well, and g) .... classical music. Oh, and I hate football! Please h) .... at corinabalcescu@netfriends.com. Thanks a lot!

b) Write a paragraph about you for NetFriends. Use the phrases in a to write about these things:

- personal information (name, age, job ...)
- things you like/don't like/love/hate
- things you do in your free time/at the weekends
- things you can do well
- any other information

Vocabulary: common adjectives

1 **a)** There are eight adjectives in the box. Find the other seven.

O	B	E	G	(N	E	W)	M	A
N	E	S	P	A	L	F	B	C
D	A	N	G	E	R	O	U	S
T	U	E	T	N	U	C	S	E
S	T	S	H	A	P	P	Y	Y
I	I	R	C	P	O	U	T	O
N	F	A	S	T	O	R	L	U
E	U	F	R	K	R	V	Z	N
P	L	N	O	B	R	S	T	G

b) Write opposites for the adjectives in **1a**.

1 *new - old*
2 ....
3 ....
4 ....
5 ....
6 ....
7 ....
8 ....

2 Which adjective is **not** correct? (Circle) the incorrect adjective.

a) a *rich/(fast)/dangerous* country
b) a/an *old/young/rich* city
c) a/an *unhappy/young/safe* person
d) a *new/happy/expensive* car
e) *fast/beautiful/poor* children
f) a *busy/dangerous/young* road
g) a/an *ugly/slow/beautiful* building

Past Simple of *be*

was/were

3 Complete the sentences about 1980 with *was* or *were*.

In 1980 ...

a) Margaret Thatcher ....*was*.... Prime Minister of Britain.
b) There .... 4.4 billion people in the world.
c) The Olympic Games .... in Moscow.
d) Bjorn Borg .... a very famous tennis player.

e) Tom Cruise .... only eighteen years old.
f) East Germany and West Germany .... different countries.
g) *The Elephant Man* and *Friday the 13th* .... popular films.
h) Jimmy Carter .... the President of the United States.

wasn't/weren't

4 **a)** Make these sentences negative.

1 He was very rich.
He wasn't very rich.
2 They were from Japan.
....
3 There was a supermarket in the square.
....
4 Their car was very expensive.
....
5 Marco's grandmother was French.
....
6 His parents were poor.
....
7 My brothers were at home last night.
....

b) Listen and check.

Questions

5 **a)** Put the words in order to make questions.

1 job - was - What - his
What was his job?
2 were - Where - from - they
.... ?
3 for class - were - late - Why - you
.... ?
4 last night - What - on TV - was
.... ?
5 you - were - Who - yesterday afternoon - with
.... ?
6 at school - Was - yesterday - Michel
.... ?
7 was - grandmother's name - your - What
.... ?
8 both your parents - Were - Russia - from
.... ?

b) Listen and check. Practise saying the questions.

was/were and *wasn't/weren't*

6 **a)** Underline the correct word to complete the text.

'My name's Niall Kelly, and I [1] *was/were* born in 1946, in a village called Mallahyde, in Ireland. My father Donald [2] *was/were* an engineer, and Maeve, my mother, [3] *was/were* a nurse. There [4] *was/were* six people in our family; my parents, my three sisters and me. My sisters [5] *was/were* usually very noisy, but I [6] *was/were* a quiet child.
I [7] *wasn't/weren't* happy at my first school.
I [8] *wasn't/weren't* good at maths or English, but I [9] *was/were* good at sport, especially football.
I remember my best friends [10] *was/were* two brothers called Jim and Adam, and they [11] *was/were* always very naughty in class! I also remember my favourite food – it [12] *was/were* hot bread!!'

b) Listen and check.

Short answers

7 **a)** Read Niall's story in Exercise 6 on page 45 again. Write short answers to these questions.

1 Was Niall born in Ireland? *Yes, he was.*
2 Was his father a doctor? ....
3 Was his mother a nurse? ....
4 Were his sisters usually noisy? ....
5 Was he happy at his first school? ....
6 Was he good at maths? ....
7 Was he good at sport? ....
8 Were Jim and Adam naughty in class? ....

b) Listen and check.

Improve your writing

Writing about the past

8 **a)** Write answers to these questions about your childhood.

Where and when were you born?

....

How many people are there in your family?

....

Were you a happy/unhappy/noisy/quiet/naughty child?

....

Were you happy at your first school?

....

What were/weren't you good at?

....

Who was your best friend?

....

What was your favourite food/book/film/game?

....

b) Write a paragraph about your childhood.

Word order

9 **a)** Put the words in brackets in the correct place.

1 Was your father born *in* London? (in)
2 This is very fast car. (a)
3 I born in Brazil in 1964. (was)
4 Were there aeroplanes in 1900? (any)
5 I usually go to cinema at the weekend. (the)
6 What time you start work? (do)
7 There were a lot of people in 1900. (poor)
8 I can play the guitar. (well)
9 Were you happy when were at school? (you)
10 Were you good sport? (at)

b) Listen and check.

Listen and read

When they were young

10

Arnold Schwarzenegger | Tony Blair | Ricky Martin

a) Match these sentences to the people. There are **four** sentences for each person.

1	He was born in Puerto Rico, in the Caribbean, in 1971.	Ricky Martin
2	He was born in 1947 in a small village near Graz, in Austria.	....
3	He was born in Edinburgh, Scotland, in May 1953.	....

4	His family was very poor, and life in Austria was difficult.	....
5	From the age of 12 to 17 he was a singer in the Latin-American pop band *Menudo*.	....
6	At school he was a happy and popular student, and was very good at English.	....

7	When he was at Oxford University he was a singer in a rock band called 'Ugly Rumours'.	....
8	His song, *La Copa de la Vida*, was the official 1998 Football World Cup song.	....
9	He loved all sport, especially bodybuilding, and in 1972 he was 'Mr Universe'.	....

10	He's now a famous Hollywood actor, and lives in the United States.	....
11	Now he's a politician, and became the British Prime Minister in 1997.	....
12	He's now a famous singer, and he can speak five languages fluently!	....

b) Listen and check your answers.

Spelling and pronunciation

Contractions

11 **a)** Write contractions: *I'm*, *you're*, *wasn't*, *doesn't* etc where possible.

1 She is from Argentina.
She's from Argentina.
2 There were not any people.
....
3 They are both doctors.
....
4 I do not like my flat.
....
5 When is your birthday?
....
6 He was not at the concert.
....
7 I cannot go to work today.
....
8 Ana does not live here.
....

b) Listen and practise saying the sentences.

Pronunciation

Years

12 **a)** How do you say these years?

1 1942 *nineteen forty-two*
2 1999 ....
3 2007 ....
4 1856 ....
5 2001 ....
6 1865 ....

b) Listen and check. Practise saying the years.

Vocabulary revision

13 Write the words and find the famous person!

a) a woman who works in the house	*h*	*o*	*u*	*s*	*e*	*w*	*i*	*f*	*e*	■
b) a very small town	■			l			g		■	■
c) the opposite of *short*	■	■	■		a			■	■	■
d) children are sometimes .... in class!	n			g			y	■	■	■
e) the opposite of *clean*	■	■	■	■	■			r		y
f) you go to a station to travel on this	■	■		r				■	■	■
g) you travel on this on the sea	■	■	■	■	■			i		■
h) the opposite of *quiet*	■	■	■	■	■		o			y
i) Victoria was the .... of England in 1900	■	■		u			n	■	■	■
j) I'm .... Do you have anything to eat?		u			r		■	■	■	■

module 10

Past Simple: irregular verbs

1 a) Write the Past Simple of these verbs in the crossword.

leave	write	become	go	sell	meet	make	have

b) Complete the sentences using the Past Simple of the verbs in **1a**.

1 Joanna ......left...... home when she was 18.
2 Last night I .... to the cinema.
3 They .... their car for £2,000.
4 Alfred Hitchcock .... 53 films in his life.
5 My father .... a book last year.
6 She .... an actress after she left school.
7 When we were children we .... a dog.
8 Erica .... her husband when she was on holiday.

c) Listen and check.

Past Simple: spelling of *-ed* endings

2 a) Write the Past Simple of these regular verbs.

1	work	..worked..	6	study	....
2	start	....	7	talk	....
3	like	....	8	want	....
4	hate	....	9	return	....
5	walk	....	10	listen	....

b) Listen and check. Practise saying the words.

Past Simple: regular verbs

3 a) Complete the sentences using the Past Simple tense of the verbs in the box.

~~live~~ work die start study watch play walk

1 My wife ...lived... in Colombia when she was young.
2 Their father .... when he was 86.
3 My grandfather .... for a British company.
4 We .... the Past Simple in class today.
5 Dylan .... computer games all night.
6 Last night I .... a really good film on TV.
7 Gabriela .... her new job two days ago.
8 It was a beautiful day, so I .... to work.

b) Listen and check.

Vocabulary: life events

4 Tick (✓) the words that match the verb, and cross (✗) the words that don't match. There is **one** wrong word for each verb.

a) **move**
- house ....✓....
- to a different country ....✓....
- a friend ....✗....

b) **get**
- a job ....
- married ....
- university ....

c) **change**
- house ....
- schools ....
- jobs ....

d) **start**
- university ....
- your partner ....
- work ....

e) **leave**
- school ....
- university ....
- married ....

f) **meet**
- your partner ....
- a good friend ....
- work ....

g) **have**
- a child ....
- a daughter ....
- married ....

Sentences in the past

5 Correct the mistakes. There is one mistake in each sentence.

a) My brother ~~were~~ *was* born in 1972.

b) We have our first child last month.

c) My daughter changed schools ago two years.

d) Tom's parents move house last year.

e) Cecilia started work after she leaved university.

f) Antonio got married on 1997.

g) I change jobs last month.

h) Charlie Chaplin maked a lot of money.

i) My husband studyed at university.

j) Was both your brothers born in Romania?

k) Tom started his new job on January.

Improve your writing

A personal history

6 **a)** Look at the information about Alicia Ojeda and complete the text.

name	Alicia Ojeda	
born	1965, Buenos Aires, Argentina	
parents	mother - housewife father - doctor	
brothers / sisters	one brother, Javier one sister, Carolina	
school	started - 1970 left - 1987	
university	yes - English and French	
first job	teacher	
partner	met Roberto - 1993	
married	yes - 1996	
children	one son, Franco	
job now	journalist	
lives now	New York	
other information	writes books; goes swimming	

Alicia Ojeda was born in a) *Buenos Aires* in 1965. Her father was a doctor and her mother was a b) .... She has one brother, Javier, and one c) .... , Carolina. She started school in d) .... , and left school in 1987. She went to university and studied e) .... and French, then she started work as a f) .... She met her partner, Roberto, in g) .... and they got married in 1996. They have one h) .... , Franco. Now Alicia works as a i) .... and lives in New York. She also writes books, and in her free time she goes j) ....

b) Complete the third column of the table for a person you know.

c) Write a paragraph about the person.

Spelling: months

7 **a)** Write the months and put them in the correct order.

1 Y A M

....

2 R E S T B P E M E

....

3 Y A N R U J A

January *1*

4 G U T A S U

....

5 M E E N B R O V

....

6 C R O O T E B

....

7 C H A R M

....

8 B E E R C E D M

....

9 U Y L J

....

10 B Y E R R A U F

....

11 P L A I R

....

12 E N U J

....

b) Listen and practise saying the months.

Listen and read

The Kennedys

8 **a)** Listen to and read the story of the Kennedy family.

The Kennedys – America's First Family

John F Kennedy is probably the most famous President in American history, but the story of the Kennedy family is not a happy one.

John was born in Boston, USA in 1917. The Kennedys were a big family, and John had five sisters and three brothers. His father, Joseph Kennedy, was a businessman, and his mother Rose was the daughter of a politician.

After university John worked as a journalist, then became a politician in 1946. But this was an unhappy time for the Kennedy family – John's brother Joe died in the Second World War, and four years later his sister Kathleen died in a plane crash.

John became a Senator* in 1952, the same year he met his wife Jacqueline Bouvier. They got married in 1953 and had three children – but their third child, Patrick, died two days after he was born.

In 1961, John F Kennedy became President, and he was very popular with the American people. He was assassinated* in Dallas, Texas in November 1963, and his brother Bobby was also assassinated five years later.

The Kennedys are a famous family, but their story is a very sad one.

* *a Senator* = a member of the American Senate * *assassinated* = killed for political reasons

b) Are these sentences true (T) or false (F)? Correct the false sentences.

1 John F Kennedy was born in ~~Washington~~ Boston. ....F....
2 Joseph and Rose Kennedy had nine children. ....
3 Two of their children died in the 1940s. ....
4 John got married three years after he became a Senator. ....
5 John and Jacqueline's third child died when he was very young. ....
6 John F Kennedy became President in 1963. ....
7 Bobby Kennedy died in 1968. ....

c) Listen and check your answers.

Prepositions

9 Complete the sentences with the prepositions in the box.

~~in~~ ~~in~~ on to on in at in on in

a) She lives ....*in*... a small town ...*in*.... Poland.
b) I was born .... December 30th 1960.
c) My father usually plays tennis .... the weekend.
d) Uli's sister left school .... 2001.
e) My next English lesson is .... Thursday.
f) I met my friend Rita .... Rome .... September.
g) We went .... the theatre .... Sunday evening.

Spelling

10 Six words are correct, six are incorrect. Tick (✓) the correct words and cross (✗) the incorrect ones. Correct the incorrect words.

a) maried ...✗.... .*married*.
b) partner ...✓.... ....
c) university ....
d) burthday ....
e) village ....
f) dificult ....
g) month ....
h) studyed ....
i) milion ....
j) musican ....
k) housewife ....
l) dirty ....

Pronunciation

11 Listen and say these words and sentences.

a) had
b) camera
c) actor
d) come
e) money
f) hungry
g) I had a camera.
h) His brother is happy.
i) I'm very hungry.
j) Do you have any money?
k) He's an actor.
l) She comes here every day.

module 11

Vocabulary: holiday expressions

1 a) Write the correct verb.

~~go~~ go to go go for stay go to go go to

1 ...*go*.... swimming
2 .... the beach
3 .... restaurants
4 .... skiing
5 .... in a hotel
6 .... museums
7 .... a walk
8 .... shopping

b) Listen and check.

Past Simple

Negative

2 a) Make these sentences negative.

1 We stayed in a hotel.
We didn't stay in a hotel.
2 They lived in Turkey.
....
3 I got home late last night.
....
4 Toshi did his homework.
....
5 Eva's father played the guitar.
....
6 My grandfather liked playing chess.
....
7 Resa worked for a computer company.
....

b) Listen and check.

yes/no questions

3

	Stephanie	Bob	Carla and Matthew
like the hotel	yes	no	yes
go to the beach	yes	yes	yes
go swimming	no	no	yes
go shopping	yes	yes	no
have a good time	yes	no	yes

a) Put the words in the correct order to make questions.

1 to the beach - Stephanie - Did - go
Did Stephanie go to the beach?
2 Did - go - swimming - Bob
.... ?
3 have - a good time - Did - Carla and Matthew
.... ?
4 the hotel - like - Bob - Did
.... ?
5 Stephanie - swimming - Did - go
.... ?
6 the hotel - Carla and Matthew - Did - like
.... ?
7 Carla and Matthew - go - Did - shopping
.... ?
8 a good time - Bob - Did - have
.... ?

b) Listen and check.

Short answers

4 Look at the table on page 54. Write short answers for the questions in Exercise 3.

a) *Yes, she did.*　　c) ....　　e) ....　　g) ....
b) ....　　d) ....　　f) ....　　h) ....

Wh- questions

5 **a)** Complete the questions about these famous people.

Indira Gandhi was born in India in 1917, and went to university in England. She got married in 1942, and became Prime Minister of India in 1966. She had two children, and died in 1984.

1 *Where* ...*did*... she ....*go*.... to university?
– In England.
2 When .... she .... married?
– In 1942.
3 .... she .... Prime Minister?
– In 1966.
4 How .... children .... ?
– Two.

Jimi Hendrix was born in the USA in 1942, and started playing the guitar when he was sixteen. He went to London in 1966 and made his first record, *Hey Joe*, in 1967. He made four albums before he died on September 18th 1970.

5 .... he .... playing the guitar?
– When he was sixteen.
6 Where .... in 1966?
– He went to London.
7 .... albums .... make?
– Four.
8 .... die?
– On September 18th 1970.

Fyodor Dostoevsky was born in Moscow in 1821, and he had six brothers and sisters. He lived in St Petersburg, and died in 1881 at the age of sixty. He wrote eight books, including *Crime and Punishment* and *The Brothers Karamazov*.

9 How .... brothers and sisters .... he .... ?
– Six.
10 Where .... ?
– In St Petersburg.
11 .... he .... ?
– In 1881.
12 How .... books .... ?
– Eight.

b) Listen and check. Practise saying the questions.

Vocabulary: time phrases

6 Put these expressions in order.

yesterday afternoon	....
ten minutes ago	....1.....
fifty years ago	....
last night	....
in 1997	....
three months ago	....
two hours ago	....2.....
last week	....
last month	....
yesterday morning	....

did, *was* and *were*

7 Circle the correct word.

a) *Did/Was/Were* you a happy child?
b) I *didn't/wasn't/weren't* study English last year.
c) Where *did/was/were* you at nine o'clock this morning?
d) What *did/was/were* you do last night?
e) Those people *didn't/wasn't/weren't* from Thailand.
f) When *did/was/were* he born?
g) Our friends *didn't/wasn't/weren't* stay in a hotel.
h) Why *did/was/were* she get up early?

Past Simple of irregular verbs

8 **a)** Write the Past Simple of these irregular verbs.

1	meet	.......met.......	6	buy	....
2	take	....	7	become	....
3	sing	....	8	come	....
4	get up	....	9	say	....
5	see	....	10	leave	....

b) Listen and check. Practise saying the words

and or *but*?

9 Put *and* or *but* in these sentences.

a) We went to New York ....but..... we didn't see the Empire State Building.
b) She left work at five o'clock .... got home at six.
c) I went to a party last night .... met some nice people.
d) Brad likes playing tennis .... he doesn't like watching it.
e) They went to Thailand on holiday .... had a great time.
f) I went to bed early .... I didn't sleep well.
g) Chris can drive a car .... he can't ride a bicycle!

Spelling

10 **a)** Put the vowels (a, e, i, o, u) in these words.

1 C H E A P
2 M _ S _ _ M
3 R _ S T _ _ R _ N T
4 B _ _ C H
5 B R _ _ K F _ S T
6 M _ _ N T _ _ N S
7 F R _ _ N D L Y
8 W _ _ T H _ R
9 B _ _ _ T _ F _ L
10 L _ N G _ _ G E
11 D _ N G _ R _ _ S
12 F R _ _ N D

b) Listen and practise the words.

Listen and read

Holiday destinations

11 **a)** Listen to and read these descriptions of two famous cities.

Vienna, the capital of Austria, is a great place for a holiday. You can visit famous buildings like the State Opera House, the Schonbrunn Palace and St Stephen's Cathedral, which is over 850 years old. Or you can go shopping along Karntner Strasse and enjoy Vienna's coffee houses, cake shops, cafés and street musicians. You can also travel along the River Danube by boat or go for a walk in the Rathauspark, one of many beautiful parks in the city. Vienna is also the home of classical music. Beethoven, Mozart and Schubert all lived there, and there are performances of their symphonies every evening. So come and stay for a weekend or a month – there's always lots to do in Vienna!

The Turkish city of Istanbul is a wonderful place to visit. In the old part of the city there are lots of interesting buildings for tourists to see, like the 500-year-old Topkapı Palace. There are also two beautiful mosques very near the Palace; the Sancta Sophia and the famous Blue Mosque.
Most visitors to Istanbul go shopping in the city's biggest market, called the 'Grand Bazaar'. There are more than four thousand shops there, and you can buy books, food, clothes, flowers and carpets. The food in Istanbul is great, and the city has some fantastic fish restaurants. So come and visit Istanbul – the city where Asia meets Europe.

b) Are these sentences true (T) or false (F)?

1 Vienna is the capital of Austria. ....T....
2 St Stephen's Cathedral is a new building. ....
3 You can drink coffee on Karntner Strasse. ....
4 You can go shopping in Rathauspark. ....
5 The Blue Mosque is in the old part of Istanbul. ....
6 There are 400 shops in the Grand Bazaar. ....
7 There are some good fish restaurants in Istanbul. ....

Improve your writing

Write an email

12 **a)** Gabriela is on holiday in Vienna. Yesterday she wrote an email to her friend Rudi. Read the email and put these words in the gaps.

~~hotel~~ dinner went shopping expensive holiday old walk boat concert city

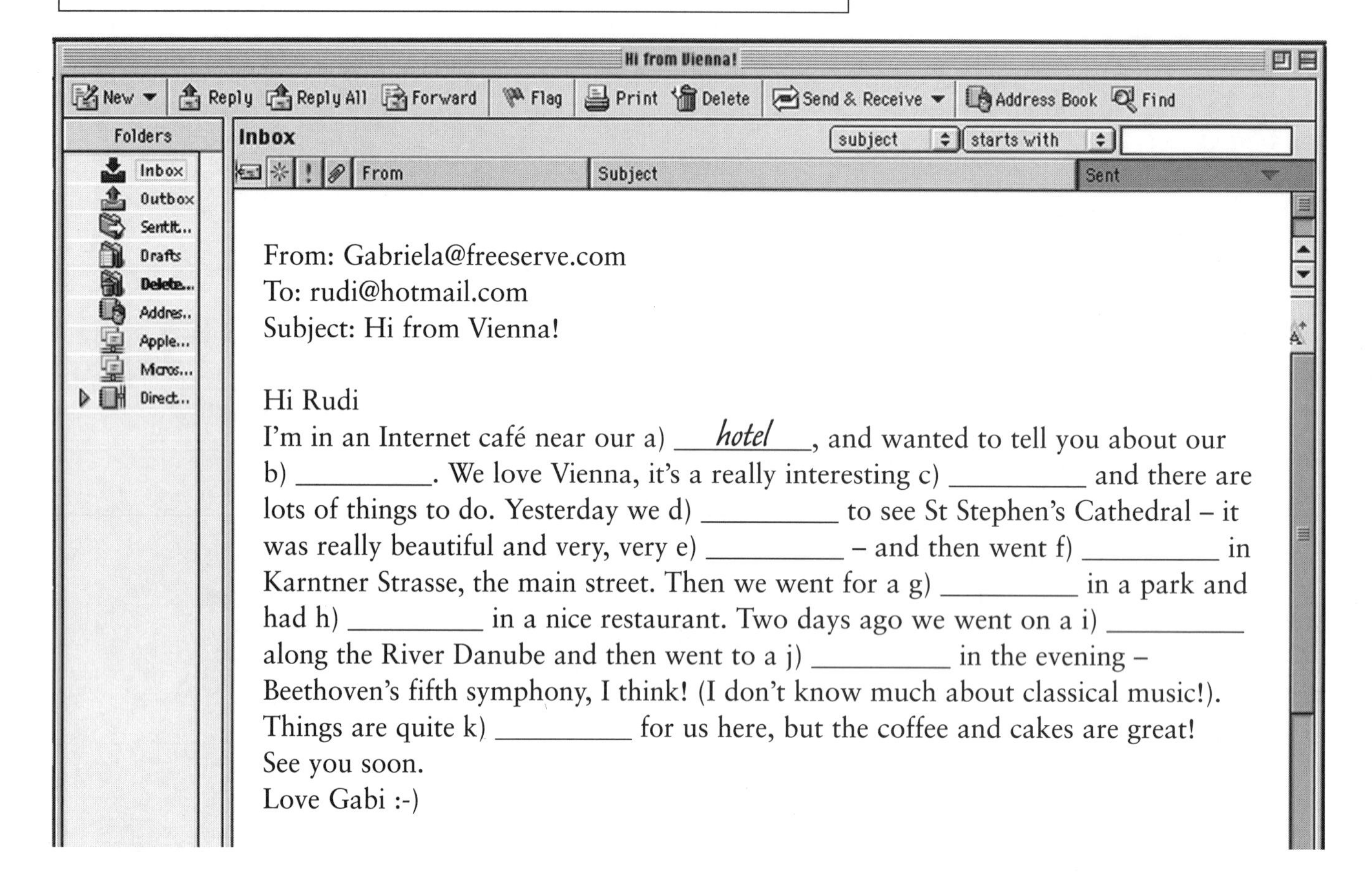

From: Gabriela@freeserve.com
To: rudi@hotmail.com
Subject: Hi from Vienna!

Hi Rudi
I'm in an Internet café near our a) __hotel__, and wanted to tell you about our b) ________. We love Vienna, it's a really interesting c) ________ and there are lots of things to do. Yesterday we d) ________ to see St Stephen's Cathedral – it was really beautiful and very, very e) ________ – and then went f) ________ in Karntner Strasse, the main street. Then we went for a g) ________ in a park and had h) ________ in a nice restaurant. Two days ago we went on a i) ________ along the River Danube and then went to a j) ________ in the evening – Beethoven's fifth symphony, I think! (I don't know much about classical music!). Things are quite k) ________ for us here, but the coffee and cakes are great!
See you soon.
Love Gabi :-)

b) Imagine you are on holiday in Istanbul or in another town or city you know. Write an email to a friend.

Pronunciation

Past Simple questions

13 Listen and say these questions.

a) Where did you stay?
b) What did she do?
c) Did you see him?
d) When did they leave?
e) Did they like her?
f) Who did he meet?
g) What did they say?
h) When did she die?

module 12

Vocabulary: things you buy

1 Complete the words.

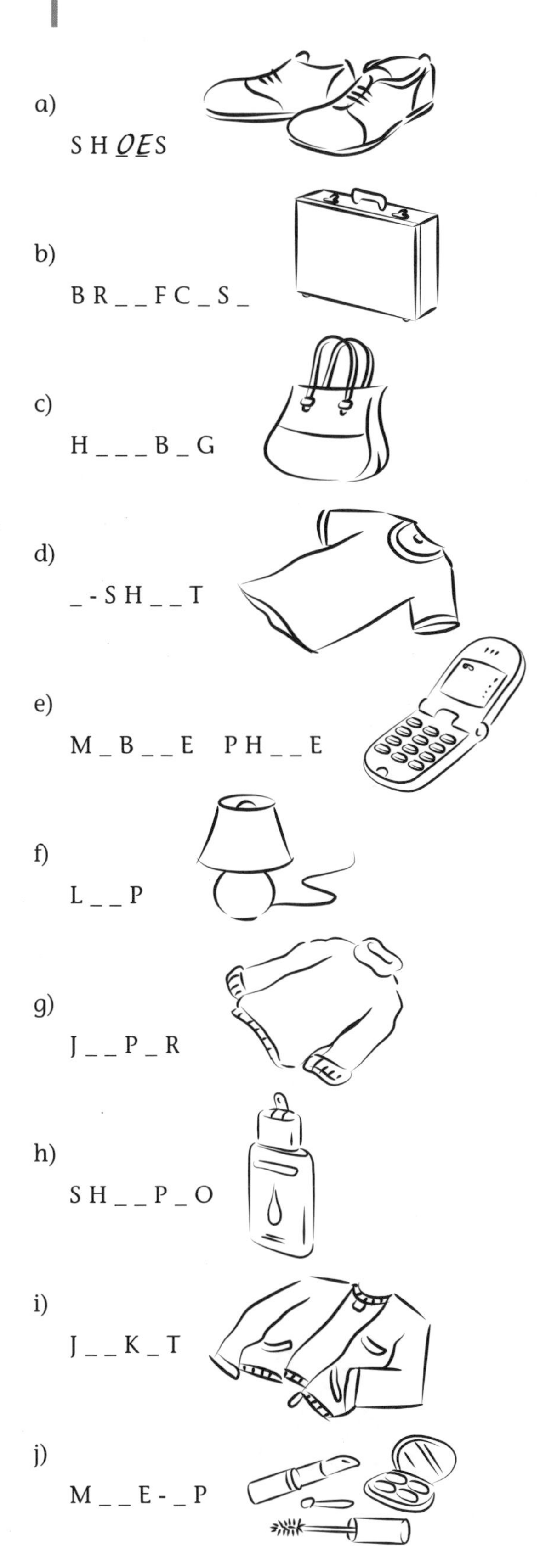

a) S H O E S

b) B R _ _ F C _ S _

c) H _ _ _ B _ G

d) _ - S H _ _ T

e) M _ B _ _ E P H _ _ E

f) L _ _ P

g) J _ _ P _ R

h) S H _ _ P _ O

i) J _ _ K _ T

j) M _ _ E - _ P

want to

2 **a)** Put these words in order.

1 tonight - I - to watch TV - want
I want to watch TV tonight.

2 furniture - don't - want - new - any - I
....

3 a film - I - to see - this afternoon - want
....

4 to go out - want - I - don't - tomorrow
....

5 after the lesson - I - a cup of coffee - want
....

6 my homework - tonight - I - to do - want - don't
....

7 my birthday - want - for - a new CD - I
....

8 to play - I - next week - want - tennis
....

b) Listen and check.

Vocabulary

Colours

3 What colour are these things? Sometimes there is more than one answer.

a) a New York taxi *yellow and black*
b) the sea ....
c) an apple ....
d) a tree ....
e) bread ....
f) a London bus ....
g) a banana ....
h) this page ....

Sizes

4 **a)** Match the questions with the answers.

1	What do you want to buy?	A	They're $16 each.
2	What size is this jumper?	B	It's brown.
3	How much is that lamp?	C	Shoes and make-up.
4	What colour are those socks?	D	It's extra large.
5	How much are these T-shirts?	E	They're size 42.
6	What colour is that jacket?	F	It's about £25.
7	What size are these shoes?	G	They're dark blue.

b) Listen and check.

going to

5 Put *am*, *are* or *is* in the gaps below. Use contractions (*'m*, *'re*, *'s*) where possible.

My husband and I a) ..are.. going to fly to Paris this weekend. He b) .... going to visit all the famous places, and I c) .... going to do lots of shopping!

Daniela

We d) .... going to visit my grandfather tomorrow – he lives in San Salvador. Our children e) .... going to stay at home with my sister.

Roberto and Gabriela

It's my birthday tomorrow, and I f) .... going to see a concert with some friends. Then we g) .... going to have dinner in a nice restaurant.

Kumiko

I h) .... going to study engineering at university next year, and my parents i) .... going to buy me a new computer.

Hussein

Positive and negative sentences

6 a) Write sentences about the future using the words below.

1 I / play tennis this weekend.
I'm going to play tennis this weekend.

2 He / not / have lunch with his sister.
He isn't going to have lunch with his sister.

3 They / see the Taj Mahal next week.
....

4 Chris / not / buy a mobile phone.
....

5 We / see a film this evening.
....

6 I / visit my friend Mark in hospital.
....

7 Margie and Vanessa / not / buy any clothes next weekend.
....

8 Luca / start a new job on Monday.
....

b) Listen and check.

Questions

7 a) Circle the correct answer, a, b or c.

1 a) Are he going to / b) Is you going to / c) Are you going to — phone Jack?

2 a) What are you going / b) What are you going to / c) What you are going to — do tonight?

3 a) Where you are going to / b) Where are you going to / c) Where's you going — go on holiday?

4 a) Are your parents going to / b) Is your parents going to / c) Your parents are going to — move house?

5 a) What's Bob going / b) What's Bob going to / c) What Bob going to — study at university?

6 a) Is she going to / b) Are she going to / c) She is going to — study English next year?

b) Listen and check.

Pronunciation

going to

8 Listen and say these sentences.

a) What's she going to do?
b) She's going to go on holiday.
c) Where's he going to go?
d) He's going to visit his aunt.
e) Are they going to study tonight?
f) No, they're going to see a film.

Missing words

9 Put these words in the sentences below.
There is one word missing in each sentence.

~~this~~ next you a to to are for

a) What are you going to do *this* evening?
b) Do you want buy a new car?
c) When you going to leave your job?
d) We don't want new teacher.
e) They're going watch a football match.
f) Are you going to do anything weekend?
g) Do you want to go a coffee?
h) What are going to do next year?

Listen and read

AIBO the electronic pet

10 a) Read and listen to this text about AIBO.

AIBO – the electronic pet

The Japanese company Sony sold the first 3,000 AIBOs on the Internet in only 20 minutes. But what exactly is an AIBO, and why do people love them so much?
An AIBO is a robot dog about 28 centimetres long, and it can do lots of amazing things. For example, it can walk, run, play with a ball, be happy or sad – just like a real dog! It can also dance, sing songs, see colours and take photographs like a camera!
A new (or 'baby') AIBO can't see or hear, but it can understand about 40 words and phrases like *How old are you?*, *Good boy* and *Don't do that*. Say its name and it answers you, say *Goodnight* and it goes to sleep. When it becomes older, the AIBO learns more words, and soon it can talk to you too. And when it's an 'adult' it can check your emails and read them to you!
These robot pets are very popular in Japan and the USA, but they aren't cheap. Each AIBO is about $2,500 – so maybe a real dog is better!

b) Are these sentences true (T) or false (F)?

1 It's from the USA. ....*F*....
2 It's very big. ....
3 It can take photographs. ....
4 New AIBOs can see and hear very well. ....
5 It can understand things people say to it. ....
6 It can check your email. ....
7 It's very expensive. ....

Improve your writing

Punctuation and capital letters

11 Put apostrophes ('), full stops (.) and capital letters (A, D, F etc) in the text.

my names sanun and i live in thailand i study engineering at university but i dont really want to be an engineer im going to travel to europe with a friend next year and then were going to work in england i cant speak english very well but my friend can i went to london when i was young but i didnt stay there for very long

Spelling

12 Write the words in the spaces and find the hidden message!

a) the Past Simple of *sell*				s	o	l	d	
b) bananas are this colour			y				o	
c) the day after *Monday*					s			y
d) I'm going to .... a new car.			u					
e) today is *Friday*, ... is *Saturday*	t		m			r		
f) you wear this when it's cold			j			p		r
g) I want something to eat. I'm		h			g			
h) tomatoes are this colour					d			
i) small, large or .... large			e				a	
j) a single or .... ticket		r				r		
k) a person sits on this					h			r
l) you give these to people in hospital		f			w		r	
m) the month after *July*						u		t
n) most vegetables are this colour			g			e		
o) What time do you .... work?					t		r	
p) What .... is this jacket? – It's a 38.	s							

Pronunciation table

Consonants		Vowels	
Symbol	Key Word	Symbol	Key Word
p	**p**et	iː	sl**ee**p
b	**b**oat	ɪ	b**i**t
t	**t**op	e	b**e**t
d	**d**o	æ	b**a**t
k	**c**at	ɑː	c**ar**
g	**g**olf	ɒ	cl**o**ck
tʃ	**ch**ur**ch**	ɔː	b**ough**t
dʒ	**j**eans	ʊ	b**oo**k
f	**f**ew	uː	b**oo**t
v	**v**iew	ʌ	b**u**t
θ	**th**irsty	ɜː	b**ir**d
ð	**th**ough	ə	broth**er**
s	**s**it	eɪ	d**ay**
z	**z**oo	əʊ	ph**o**ne
ʃ	fre**sh**	aɪ	b**y**
ʒ	lei**s**ure	aʊ	n**ow**
h	**h**at	ɔɪ	b**oy**
m	**m**other	ɪə	d**ear**
n	su**n**	eə	h**air**
ŋ	you**ng**	ʊə	d**oor**
l	**l**ot		
r	**r**un		
j	**y**es		
w	**w**et		

Answer key

module 1

Names and introductions

1 a)

2 Are you Teresa Daley?
3 Hello. What's your name?
4 A: Hello, my name's Frank.
B: Hi, I'm Paola. Nice to meet you.

Vocabulary: jobs; *a/an*

2

b) a doctor
c) a student
d) an actor
e) a businessman
f) an engineer
g) a police officer
h) a teacher

he/she/his/her

3 a)

2 His 3 He 4 She 5 Her 6 Her 7 Her 8 She
9 His 10 He

I/my/you/your/his/her

4

2 c 3 a 4 a 5 a 6 a

The alphabet; *How do you spell ...?*

6

b) Catherine Zeta-Jones
c) Juliet Binoche
d) Jodie Foster
e) Quentin Tarantino
f) Kevin Spacey

7 a)

2 What's his
3 How do you
4 What's her first
5 What's her full

Numbers 0–20

8 a)

11 9 17 12 6 18 10 4 5

8 b)

seven eight thirteen two sixteen
fourteen twenty fifteen nineteen

Improve your writing

Full stops, question marks

9

b) 'Are you Anna Schmidt?'
No, I'm Barbara Schmidt.'
c) 'Hi, Sonja! How are you?'
'I'm fine. And you?'
d) 'What's her surname?'
e) 'His name's Jan Talich. He's a doctor.'
f) 'What's your job?'
'I'm a singer.'

Capital letters (1)

10

b) Johnny Depp is an actor.
c) Her name is Jennifer Jones. She's a singer.
d) A: 'What's your name?
B: 'My name's Andrea.'
e) 'Hello, Abdul, how are you?'
'I'm fine.'
f) My name's Istvan and I'm an engineer.

Listen and read

11

Caryn Johnson's real name is Whoopi Goldberg.

module 2

Vocabulary: countries

1

b) Brazil
c) Japan
d) Italy
e) USA
f) Turkey
g) France
h) Poland
i) Spain
j) Russia

be with *I* and *you*

2 a)

2 I'm Francesca. Nice to meet you.
3 Where are you from?
4 I'm from Italy.
5 Are you from Rome?
6 No, I'm from Milan.
7 Are you a student?
8 No, I'm your teacher.

Negatives

3

b) You're not from London
c) You're not a teacher.
d) I'm not a teacher.
e) I'm not from a big country.
f) You're not from Russia.

Nationalities

4 a)

2 She's American.
3 He's Japanese.
4 She's French.
5 He's Italian.
6 She's Turkish.
7 She's Russian.
8 He's Spanish.

is/are/am

5

b) Am c) Is d) Are e) am f) Are g) is h) Is

Questions

6

b) Are you from Australia?
c) Is Budapest in Hungary?
d) Are you 18?
e) Is your name Claudia?
f) Is he French?
g) Is it a Japanese car?
h) Is Edinburgh the capital of Scotland?

Numbers 21–100

7

b) twenty-three c) sixty-four d) eighty-nine
e) twenty-seven f) fifty-eight g) seventy-eight h) ninety

Improve your writing

Writing about yourself

8 a)

2 My 3 'm 4 from 5 student 6 email
7 single 8 Please

Ages

10 a)

2 He's from Sydney, Australia.
3 He's twenty-six.

10 c)

2 Where is she from?
3 How old is she?

10 e)

2 His surname's Zmuda.
3 Where is he from?

10 g)

1 She's forty-one.
2 What's her surname?
3 She's from São Paulo, Brazil.

Capital letters (2)

11

b) Warsaw is the capital city of Poland.
c) Where is Virginia from? I think she's Argentinian.
d) Osaka is a big city in Japan.
e) I'm 21 and I'm Russian.

Question words

12

b) How c) What d) Where e) How f) What
g) How h) Where

module 3

Vocabulary: nouns

1

b) a woman c) a child d) a car e) a bus f) a house
g) a shop

Plural nouns

2

b) buses c) children d) people e) cities f) men
g) women h) countries

be: plural

3

b) Is c) are d) is e) are f) is

Opposites

4 a)

2 cold 3 hot 4 small 5 big 6 expensive

be with *we* and *they*

5

b) aren't, they
c) Are, we
d) aren't
e) are, we
f) aren't, they
g) are
h) we

we're/they're/our/their

6 a)

2 – e 3 – b 4 – d 5 – c 6 – a

Spelling

7

3 number 4 ✓ 5 cities 6 ✓ 7 expensive 8 ✓
9 beautiful 10 children 11 married 12 ✓

Food and drink vocabulary

8

2 eggs 3 cheese 4 meat 5 vegetables 6 bread 7 fish
8 coffee 9 milk 10 water 11 pasta 12 fruit

this/that/these/those

9

b) those c) that d) those e) this f) those g) that

Prepositions

10

b) on c) at d) in e) in f) from g) in

Improve your writing

A postcard

13

b) How
c) We're here
d) in a hotel
e) expensive
f) beautiful
g) are very good
h) See you

module 4

Vocabulary: places in a town

1

b) bus stop
c) restaurant
d) station
e) car park
f) supermarket
g) square

Prepositions

2 a)

2 on
3 the right
4 the station
5 of the restaurant
6 in

there is/there are

3 a)

2 There are 3 There's 4 There are 5 There's 6 There's
7 There are 8 There are 9 There's

Negative sentences

4 a)

2 There aren't any Indian restaurants.
3 There isn't a railway station.
4 There aren't any Internet cafés.
5 There isn't a library
6 There aren't any beaches.

Questions

5 a)

2 Are there any good shops?
3 Is there a university?
4 Is there a bus station?
5 Are there any interesting bars?
6 Is there a cinema?

All forms

6

b) – 3 c) – 6 d) – 1 e) – 4 f) – 2

some, *any* and *a*

7

b) some c) any d) a e) any f) a g) a h) some

Common adjectives

8

b) interesting c) quiet d) famous e) busy f) small g) nice

Listen and read

9 b)

2 In the Italian pavilion.
3 In the French pavilion.
4 In the United Kingdom pavilion.
5 In the Japanese pavilion.
6 In the Moroccan pavilion.

Improve your writing

Capital letters (revision)

10

b) 'Is Andrea Bocelli Spanish?'
'No, he's Italian.'
c) London is the capital city of England. There's also a London in Canada and two in the United States!
d) There are two official languages in Canada – French and English.
e) Spanish is the official language in Argentina, Chile and Uruguay – but in Brazil the official language is Portuguese.

is or *are?*

11 a)

2 are 3 are 4 is 5 Are 6 is

module 5

Family vocabulary

1 a)

2 wife 3 children 4 daughter 5 son

1 c)

7 sister 8 parents 9 mother 10 father

1 e)

12 grandfather 13 grandmother 14 grandchildren
15 granddaughter 16 grandson

Possessive 's

2

b) What's your sister's name?
c) John's brother is a footballer.
d) There's a party at Frank's house!
e) 'Is this your book?' 'No, it's Barbara's.'
f) Jackie is Catherine's sister.
g) Our dog's name is Max.

's – *is* or possessive?

3

c) *is* d) possessive e) possessive f) *is* g) possessive h) *is*

Verbs

4

b) live c) work d) have

Present Simple

Negative

5

b) I don't study French.
c) I don't work in the centre of town.
d) I don't have a brother.
e) We don't live in Poland.
f) Our children don't drink tea.

Questions

6 a)

2 Do you study German?
3 Do you have any children?
4 Do you live in a town or a city?
5 Do you have any pets?
6 Do you have any brothers and sisters?

Short answers

7 a)

3 Yes, I do. 5 Yes, I do.
4 No, I don't. 6 No, I don't.

Question words: *How*, *What*, *Where*, *Who*

8

b) Where c) How d) Who e) How f) Where

Personal possessions

9

b) money c) mobile phone d) watch e) magazine
f) glasses g) radio h) purse i) wallet j) camera
k) credit card

Improve your writing

Writing about your family

10

2 with 5 brother's 8 name, she is
3 don't, my 6 their
4 are 7 grandparents

Prepositions

11

b) in c) with d) with e) for f) with g) in, in

Articles

12

b) 'I work for a German bank.'
c) 'I'm a medical student.'
d) 'There are a lot of people in my flat!'
e) 'We're a big family.'
f) 'I have four brothers and a sister.'
g) 'We have a nice big house.'

Listen and read

14 b)

1 13 2 11 3 18 4 500 5 32 6 7

module 6

Vocabulary: likes and dislikes

1 a)

2 'I love Robbie Williams.'
3 'I don't like cooking.'
4 'Classical music is OK.'
5 'I hate football.'

Object pronouns

2

b) it c) her d) him e) it f) them g) it

Vocabulary: useful nouns

3

b) games, football
c) television, cartoons
d) computers, Internet
e) coffee, tea
f) supermarket

Present Simple: *he* and *she*

4

b) uses c) watches d) works e) reads f) teaches g) lives h) plays i) has

Present Simple

Questions

6 a)

2 Does Tina drink a lot of coffee? No, she doesn't.
Does Tony drink a lot of coffee? Yes, he does.
3 Does Tina like rock music? No, she hates it.
Does Tony like rock music? Yes, he does.
4 Does Tina like dancing? Yes, she does.
Does Tony like dancing? No, he doesn't.
5 Does Tina study a foreign language? Yes, she does.
Does Tony study a foreign language? No, he doesn't.
6 Does Tina speak French? Yes, she does.
Does Tony speak French? No, he doesn't.
7 Does Tina play a sport? Yes, she plays tennis.
Does Tony play a sport? No, he doesn't.
8 Does Tina like computer games? No, she doesn't.
Does Tony like computer games? Yes, he loves them.

Negative

7

b) Paul doesn't teach English.
c) Carla doesn't live with her parents.
d) My father doesn't like rock music.
e) Sam doesn't play tennis.
f) Olga doesn't work for a British company.
g) Brian doesn't speak Japanese.

All forms

8

b) works, speak, speaks
c) play, doesn't, watches
d) doesn't, eats
e) teaches, like
f) likes, doesn't, hates
g) Does, does, loves

Improve your writing

Using pronouns

9 a)

2 city 3 Her 4 He's 5 He 6 live 7 They 8 their

Listen and read

Famous couples

10 b)

2 He is from Philadelphia, USA.
3 His wife's name is Jada Pinkett Smith.
4 Their children's names are Jaden and Willow.
5 They live in Los Angeles.

10 d)

2 Where is she from?
3 Is she married?
4 Do they have any children?
5 Where do they live?

module 7

Daily routines

1 a)

2 go 3 have 4 start 5 have 6 finish 7 get 8 have 9 go 10 sleep

Present Simple

Questions

2 a)

2 When does she go to work?
3 Where does she have breakfast?
4 What time does she start work?
5 Does she have a big lunch?
6 When does she finish work?
7 What time does she get home?
8 Does she go to bed early?

All forms

3 a)

2 doesn't, start
3 Does, work
4 finish
5 do, have
6 don't, go
7 Does, have
8 sleeps

Vocabulary: days of the week

4

b) Wednesday 3 c) Thursday 4 d) Sunday 7 e) Saturday 6 f) Tuesday 2 g) Friday 5

Adverbs of frequency

5 a)

2 always 3 never 4 not usually 5 sometimes

5 b)

1 always 3 sometimes 4 not usually 5 never

Word order with adverbs

6 a)

2 I don't usually play tennis at the weekend.
3 My brother and I always play football at the weekend.
4 Shops in our town sometimes open at night.
5 Barbara doesn't usually work on Mondays.
6 I usually listen to music when I get home.
7 Children in Britain never go to school on Sundays.
8 We always go to work by train

Verbs and nouns

7

b) clean c) meet d) go to e) do f) watch g) read h) listen to i) go

Time expressions

8 a)

2 at 3 Ø 4 at, on 5 in 6 Ø 7 at, in 8 at, on

Telling the time

9

b) twenty-five past eleven
c) ten past nine
d) five to four
e) ten to twelve
f) half past two
g) quarter to six
h) quarter past five

Listen and read

Life in Britain today

10 b)

1 fish and chips 2 go swimming 3 3 hours 4 Spain

Improve your writing

Personal descriptions

11 a)

He's 28 and he's a <u>computer engineer</u>. On Monday evenings he <u>has a violin lesson</u>, and on Thursday afternoons he <u>plays tennis with his brother</u>. On Friday evenings, he usually <u>has dinner in a restaurant</u> and he sometimes <u>goes to a club</u>. At the weekend he <u>always gets up late</u> and he <u>sometimes goes to a friend's house in the</u> afternoon..

Spelling

Double letters

12

The correct spellings are:
b) really c) always d) usually e) travel f) cooking g) shopping h) cigarette i) finish j) coffee

module 8

Action verbs

1

b) sit c) hear d) play e) see f) swim g) ride h) walk i) talk j) run

can and *can't*

2 a)

2 Can 3 can't 4 Can 5 can't 6 Can 7 can't 8 can

Short answers

3 a)

2 No, they can't.
3 No, he can't.
4 Yes, she can.
5 No, I can't.
6 Yes, he can.
7 Yes, they can.

Vocabulary: parts of the body

4

b) eye c) ear d) hand e) blood f) arm g) leg h) foot i) bone

Vocabulary: quantities

5

b) metres, seconds c) centimetres d) hours e) kilos f) kilometres g) days h) litres i) minutes

Questions

Question words

6 a)

2 When 3 Why 4 Who 5 Where 6 How many

6 b)

2 – E 3 – F 4 – B 5 – D 6 – A

Forming questions

7 a)

2 Where does your brother live?
3 What's the capital of Colombia?
4 Who's your favourite singer?
5 Why do you study English?
6 When do you usually go to the cinema?
7 How many languages does Monica speak?

Big numbers

8 a)

2 three million
3 two thousand five hundred
4 three hundred and sixty-five
5 one hundred thousand
6 seven hundred
7 nine thousand, nine hundred and ninety-nine

Listen and read
Living in the Antarctic

9 b)

1 He is an engineer.
2 -20° C
3 12
4 He goes swimming in the sea.
5 He plays volleyball or watches videos.
6 Yes, he does.

Spelling: 'silent' letters

10

2 mountain 3 Wednesday 4 interesting 5 vegetables
6 wrong 7 foreign language 8 daughter 9 listen
10 guitar

Improve your writing
Describing yourself

11

b) I live in
c) I also study
d) In my free time
e) I usually
f) I can
g) I love
h) write to me

module 9

Vocabulary: common adjectives

1 a)

dangerous, happy, beautiful, young, fast, busy, poor

1 b)

dangerous – safe happy – unhappy beautiful – ugly
young – old fast – slow busy – calm poor – rich

2

The incorrect adjectives are:
b) young c) safe d) happy e) fast f) young g) slow

Past Simple of *be*
was/were

3

b) were c) were d) was e) was f) were g) were h) was

wasn't/weren't

4 a)

2 They weren't from Japan.
3 There wasn't a supermarket in the square.
4 Their car wasn't very expensive.
5 Marco's grandmother wasn't French.
6 His parents weren't poor.
7 My brothers weren't at home last night.

Questions

5 a)

2 Where were they from?
3 Why were you late for class?
4 What was on TV last night?
5 Who were you with yesterday afternoon?
6 Was Michel at school yesterday?
7 What was your grandmother's name?
8 Were both your parents from Russia?

was/were and *wasn't/weren't*

6 a)

2 was 3 was 4 were 5 were 6 was 7 wasn't
8 wasn't 9 was 10 were 11 were 12 was

Short answers

7 a)

2 No, he wasn't.
3 Yes, she was.
4 Yes, they were.
5 No, he wasn't.
6 No, he wasn't.
7 Yes, he was.
8 Yes, they were.

Word order

9 a)

2 This is a very fast car.
3 I was born in Brazil in 1964.
4 Were there any aeroplanes in 1900?
5 I usually go to the cinema at the weekend.
6 What time do you start work?
7 There were a lot of poor people in 1900.
8 I can play the guitar well.
9 Were you happy when you were at school?
10 Were you good at sport?

Listen and read
When they were young

10 a)

2 Arnold Schwarzenegger
3 Tony Blair
4 Arnold Schwarzenegger
5 Ricky Martin
6 Tony Blair
7 Tony Blair
8 Ricky Martin
9 Arnold Schwarzenegger
10 Arnold Schwarzenegger
11 Tony Blair
12 Ricky Martin

Spelling and pronunciation
Contractions

11 a)

2 There weren't any people.
3 They're both doctors.
4 I don't like my flat.
5 When's your birthday?
6 He wasn't at the concert.
7 I can't go to work today.
8 Ana doesn't live here.

Pronunciation
Years

12 a)

2 nineteen ninety-nine
3 two thousand and seven
4 eighteen fifty-six
5 two thousand and one
6 eighteen sixty-five

Vocabulary revision

13

b) village c) tall d) naughty e) dirty f) train g) ship
h) noisy i) queen j) hungry
The famous person is: Walt Disney

module 10

Past Simple: irregular verbs

1 a)

1 sold 2 became 3 had 4 wrote/went 5 made
6 met 7 left

1 b)

2 went 3 sold 4 made 5 wrote 6 became
7 had 8 met

Past Simple: spelling of *-ed* endings

2 a)

2 started 3 liked 4 hated 5 walked 6 studied
7 talked 8 wanted 9 returned 10 listened

Past Simple: regular verbs

3 a)

2 died 3 worked 4 studied 5 played 6 watched
7 started 8 walked

Vocabulary: life events

4

The **wrong** words are:
b) university c) house d) your partner e) married
f) work g) married

Sentences in the past

5

b) We <u>had</u> our first child last month.
c) My daughter changed schools two years <u>ago</u>.
d) Tom's parents <u>moved</u> house last year.
e) Cecilia started work after she <u>left</u> university.
f) Antonio got married <u>in</u> 1997.
g) I <u>changed</u> jobs last month.
h) Charlie Chaplin <u>made</u> a lot of money.
i) My husband <u>studied</u> at university.
j) <u>Were</u> both your brothers born in Romania?
k) Tom started his new job <u>in</u> January.

Improve your writing

A personal history

6 a)

b) housewife c) sister d) 1970 e) English f) teacher
g) 1993 h) son i) journalist j) swimming

Spelling: months

7 a)

1 May 5 2 September 9 3 January 1 4 August 8
5 November 11 6 October 10 7 March 3 8 December 12
9 July 7 10 February 2 11 April 4 12 June 6

Listen and read

The Kennedys

8 b)

2 T
3 T
4 False. John got married one year after he became a Senator.
5 T
6 False. John F Kennedy became President in 1961.
7 T

Prepositions

9

b) on c) at d) in e) on f) in, in g) to, on

Spelling

10

c) ✓ d) birthday e) ✓ f) difficult g) ✓ h studied
i) million j) musician k) ✓ l) ✓

module 11

Vocabulary: holiday expressions

1 a)

2 go to 3 go to 4 go 5 stay 6 go to 7 go for 8 go

Past Simple

Negative

2 a)

2 They didn't live in Turkey.
3 I didn't get home late last night.
4 Toshi didn't do his homework.
5 Eva's father didn't play the guitar.
6 My grandfather didn't like playing chess.
7 Resa didn't work for a computer company.

yes/no questions

3 a)

2 Did Bob go swimming?
3 Did Carla and Matthew have a good time?
4 Did Bob like the hotel?
5 Did Stephanie go swimming?
6 Did Carla and Matthew like the hotel?
7 Did Carla and Matthew go shopping?
8 Did Bob have a good time?

Short answers

4

b) No, he didn't.
c) Yes, they did.
d) No, he didn't.
e) No, she didn't.
f) Yes, they did.
g) No, they didn't.
h) No, he didn't.

Wh- questions

5 a)

2 When did she get married?
3 When did she become Prime Minister?
4 How many children did she have?
5 When did he start playing the guitar?
6 Where did he go in 1966?
7 How many albums did he make?
8 When did he die?
9 How many brothers and sisters did he have?
10 Where did he live?
11 When did he die?
12 How many books did he write?

Vocabulary: time phrases

6

ten minutes ago
two hours ago
last night
yesterday afternoon
yesterday morning
last week
last month
three months ago
in 1997
fifty years ago

did, *was* and *were*

7

b) didn't c) were d) did e) weren't f) was g) didn't h) did

Past Simple of irregular verbs

8 a)

2 took 3 sang 4 got up 5 saw 6 bought 7 became 8 came 9 said 10 left

and or *but*?

9

b) and c) and d) but e) and f) but g) but

Spelling

10 a)

2 museum 3 restaurant 4 beach 5 breakfast 6 mountains 7 friendly 8 weather 9 beautiful 10 language 11 dangerous 12 friend

Listen and read

Holiday destinations

11 b)

2 F 3 T 4 F 5 T 6 F 7 T

Improve your writing

Write an email

12 a)

b) holiday c) city d) went e) old f) shopping g) walk h) dinner i) boat j) concert k) expensive

module 12

Vocabulary: things you buy

1

b) briefcase c) handbag d) T-shirt e) mobile phone f) lamp g) jumper h) shampoo i) jacket j) make-up

want to

2 a)

2 I don't want any new furniture.
3 I want to see a film this afternoon.
4 I don't want to go out tomorrow.
5 I want a cup of coffee after the lesson.
6 I don't want to do my homework tonight.
7 I want a new CD for my birthday.
8 I want to play tennis next week.

Vocabulary

Colours

3

b) blue, green and grey
c) red and green
d) green and brown
e) brown and white
f) red
g) yellow and brown
h) black and white

Sizes

4 a)

2 – D 3 – F 4 – G 5 – A 6 – B 7 – E

going to

5

b) 's c) 'm d) 're e) are f) 'm g) 're h) 'm i) are

Positive and negative sentences

6 a)

3 They're going to see the Taj Mahal next week.
4 Chris isn't going to buy a mobile phone.
5 We're going to see a film this evening.
6 I'm going to visit my friend Mark in hospital.
7 Margie and Vanessa aren't going to buy any clothes next weekend.
8 Luca is going to start a new job on Monday.

Questions

7 a)

2 – b 3 – b 4 – a 5 – b 6 – a

Missing words

9

b) Do you want to buy a new car?
c) When are you going to leave your job?
d) We don't want a new teacher.
e) They're going to watch a football match.
f) Are you going to do anything next weekend?
g) Do you want to go for a coffee?
h) What are you going to do next year?

Listen and read

AIBO the electronic pet

10 b)

2 F 3 T 4 F 5 T 6 T 7 T

Improve your writing

Punctuation and capital letters

11

My name's Sanun and I live in Thailand. I study engineering at university but I don't really want to be an engineer. I'm going to travel to Europe with a friend next year and then we're going to work in England. I can't speak English very well but my friend can. I went to London when I was young but I didn't stay there for very long.

Spelling

12

b) yellow c) Tuesday d) buy e) tomorrow f) jumper g) hungry h) red i) extra j) return k) chair l) flowers m) August n) green o) start p) size

The hidden message is: *see you next course*